Buddhism of the Heart

BUDDHISM
OF THE
HEART

Reflections on **Shin Buddhism**
and Inner Togetherness

JEFF WILSON
Foreword by **Mark Unno** and **Taitetsu Unno**

WISDOM PUBLICATIONS • BOSTON

Wisdom Publications
199 Elm Street
Somerville MA 02144 USA
www.wisdompubs.org

Library of Congress Cataloging-in-Publication Data
Wilson, Jeff (Jeff Townsend)
 Buddhism of the heart : reflections on Shin Buddhism and inner togetherness / Jeff Wilson ; foreword by Mark Unno and Taitetsu Unno.
   p. cm.
 Includes bibliographical references and index.
 ISBN 0-86171-583-7 (pbk. : alk. paper)
 1. Religious life--Shin (Sect) I. Title.
 BQ8736.W56 2009
 294.3'926--dc22
                          2009006563

13 12 11 10 09
5 4 3 2 1

Cover design by Phil Pascuzzo. Interior design by Tony Lulek. Set in Bulmer MT Regular 12/16.

"This World of Dew" from *Dew on the Grass: The Life and Poetry of Kobayashi Issa* by Makoto Ueda. Leiden: Brill, 2004. Reprinted with permission

"Insects on a Branch" from *Dusk Lingers: Haiku of Issa*. Translated by Dennis Maloney. Pittsburg, PA: The Lilliput Review, 2006. Reprinted with permission

Issa poems on pages 105, 161, 199, 208, and 209 from *Haiku of Kobayashi Issa*. Translated by David G. Lanoue, haikuguy.com/issa, 1991–2008. Reprinted with permission

Wisdom Publications' books are printed on acid-free paper and meet the guidelines for permanence and durability of the Production Guidelines for Book Longevity of the Council on Library Resources.

Printed in the United States of America.

This book was produced with environmental mindfulness. We have elected to print this title on 30% PCW recycled paper. As a result, we have saved the following resources: 12 trees, 9 million BTUs of energy, 1,082 lbs. of greenhouse gases, 4,490 gallons of water, and 577 lbs. of solid waste. For more information, please visit our website, www.wisdompubs.org. This paper is also FSC certified. For more information, please visit www.fscus.org.

Dedicated to
Reverend Taitetsu Unno, Reverend T. Kenjitsu Nakagaki,
and Reverend Fumiaki Usuki
and to
the wonderful people of the New York Buddhist Church,
American Buddhist Study Center, and West Los Angeles
Buddhist Temple

I will tell you something about stories[...]
They aren't just entertainment.
Don't be fooled.
They are all we have, you see,
all we have to fight off
illness and death.
You don't have anything
if you don't have the stories
—Leslie Marmon Silko, *Ceremony*

Table of Contents

Foreword

by Mark Unno and Taitetsu Unno

As Buddhism in the West continues to evolve, significant but relatively unknown expressions of the Dharma continue to come to light. Among them is Jodo Shinshu, or Shin Buddhism as it has come to be known in English, the stream of Japanese Pure Land tradition that originated from India, made its way across Korea, China, and then on to Japan. In East Asia, Pure Land communities grew into a broad and vast river that eventually came to encompass one of the largest bodies of practice. Although it made its first appearance in the West in the late nineteenth century, practices devoted to Amida Buddha are only now becoming more widely recognized here.

As a stream within Mahayana Buddhism, Shin's Pure Land Buddhist thought—as articulated by its founder Shinran Shonin—subscribes to the two-fold truth of form and emptiness, of words and the truth beyond words. This is regarded as a "twofold" truth rather than two separate truths—much like the two sides of the same coin. The truth of form and of words belongs to the world of appearances.

Thus, when we see a tree, we see "green," "willowy," "shade," "photosynthesis," and so forth. These concepts all describe the truth of form through words and concepts, and Shin—like Buddhism generally—does not deny this reality. And yet, there is a deeper truth that discloses itself only when one empties the mind of these ideas. That is the truth of *emptiness*, the oneness of reality that lies beyond categories. It is the flow of reality as it is beyond words, before conceptualization, things just as they are in their "thusness" or "suchness." This is true not only for the things of this world such as trees and grasses but also in our relationships with other people. A stranger who we may have a negative initial impression of, once we get to know them beyond our preconceptions, often turns out to be someone very much like ourselves, with similar fears, concerns, joys, and hopes. But we will never know this as long as we prejudge or pigeonhole them into the categories of our own making.

Form and language, then, are not negative or problems in and of themselves. It is only when we become dogmatically attached to them, or when we insist on seeing the world through a preconceived filter, our "rose-colored glasses," that we run into trouble and cause suffering to others as well as to ourselves. Yet, the moment that we are led to recognize our prejudices, dogmatism, and rigidity, and we are able to see ourselves with a bit more humor and humility, we have already begun to let go into the great flow of emptiness, oneness, and suchness, where we are in intimate kinship with all beings and things.

Within Shin Buddhist communities, such concepts as *blind passion*, *foolish being*, and *boundless compassion* have become part of the English-language vocabulary of Pure Land practice. Nonetheless, many people—even readers of Western Buddhism—may not yet be familiar with these terms, so brief explanations of a few key terms may be in order here.

In Shin, the person who is entrapped in the mental prison of his own making is said to be caught in his own "blind passions." Passions and desires, like words and concepts, are also not negative in and of themselves. It is only when we become obsessed by our ideas about what we think we are or should be that we become blind to the reality before us. Just as love must be allowed to unfold and cannot be forced, our broader experience of life and death can only truly unfold in the freedom of mutual encounter between us and the world, when we are no longer merely blinded by our desire to force things into a mold that has been pre-made in our minds.

This encounter with reality, the realization of emptiness, is described in Shin Buddhism as the embrace of boundless compassion. Although emptiness, being beyond all distinctions, is formless and characterless, the experience of being released from the suffering of our blind passions into the vast, ocean-like emptiness is nonetheless experienced as a positive realization. *Compassion* comes from the Latin *com-* meaning "with," and *passion*, "feeling." Thus, "compassion" is "feeling with" the flow of reality, a compassion that is boundless because it is beyond categorization, ineffable, inconceivable.

The one who is filled with blind passions is called a "foolish being," and the embodiment of boundless compassion is said to be Amida Buddha. This corresponds to the Sanskrit Amitabha Buddha which means the "Buddha of Infinite Light" (alternately, Amitayus Buddha, "the Buddha of Eternal Life"). Yet, since boundless compassion is always unfolding and never static, it would be more precise to render Amida Buddha as "the awakening of infinite light." Just as we experience a palpable darkness when we are troubled and a countervailing clarity or illumination when we are freed from our worries, the realization of emptiness comes to us as a vivid sense of limitless light.

Blind passion and boundless compassion, foolish being and Amida Buddha: these are terms of awakening in the daily religious life of the Shin Buddhist. Furthermore, these polar pairs are captured in the central practice of Shin Buddhism, which is to speak or chant the Name of Amida Buddha, which is known in terms of the six-syllable phrase, "Namu Amida Butsu"—literally, "I entrust myself to the awakening of infinite light." This phrase is called the *nembutsu*.

Even though blind passions bind us, we can never get rid of them entirely, as long as we live in this limited mind and body that we call the "self." In the moment of release from our ego-prison, we may feel the deep impetus to never complain again, to never pre-judge others again. And yet, we do complain; we still prejudge. However, once we have been awakened to the working of Amida's boundless compassion, each moment of ignorance and blind passion becomes another opportunity to gain insight and learn anew. Thus, in Shin Buddhism, we greatly value our blind passions as the very source of our own wisdom and compassion. It is only through recognizing our mistakes that we learn and grow; our blind passions are like fertilizer for the field of our own spiritual development. Blind passions and boundless compassion go hand-in-hand; the deeper we go into the ocean of boundless compassion, the more we realize our foolishness.

This is our dance with reality, and with ourselves, the rhythm and song of "*Namu*" our foolishness and "*Amida Butsu*" the wellspring of boundless compassion that arises from our own deepest, truest reality. Ultimately, even the nembutsu arises not from ourselves, from our own ego, but is experienced as the call from the deepest level of reality, from the depths of our own being, in which the flow of emptiness/oneness is realized in each manifestation of form and appearance. The movement of boundless compassion is also known as the Vow of Amida, the realization of the vow to bring all beings to the realization of oneness. The nembutsu expresses our receiving this deep vow to liberate and realize oneness with all beings.

Yet, this kind of philosophical explanation can only take one so far. And so, alongside the profound philosophical works of Shin Buddhism composed by Shinran Shonin and others, diverse genres of literature also evolved, in some ways less systematic but no less enriching. These include the stories and observations of ordinary Pure Land followers that have been collected down through the ages in what has come to be known as *setsuwa*, or folk literature, and other sources such as memoirs, essays, and biographies.

As Jeff Wilson notes in the present work, in the late nineteenth and early twentieth centuries, the poems and stories of the *myokonin*, the "wondrous persons" of the Shin tradition conveyed the lives and reflections of ordinary followers, of peasants and craftspeople with little or no formal education. And in contemporary Japan, there has been a proliferation of memoirs, biographies, and essays, most of which have yet to be rendered into Western languages.

Although few in number and little known, we do have examples of such literature in English. These include Shinmon Aoki's *Coffinman: The Journal of a Buddhist Mortician*, the memoir of a contemporary lay Shin follower translated from the Japanese. In terms of works that were composed in English for Western audiences from the beginning, there are such Dharma talk collections as Gyomay Kubose's *Everyday Suchness* and Hozen Seki's *Great Natural Way: Pure Land Dharma Lectures, Sermons and Sayings*. Yet while the lives of ordinary Shin followers are conveyed through these works, they are presented through the lens of full-time ministers who tended to their congregations.

Kenneth Tanaka's *Ocean: An Introduction to Jodo-Shinshu Buddhism in America* is a work that helps to make Shin teachings accessible to Western audiences. It contains both ideas and stories and in that sense points to understanding that brings doctrine to life through experience. It reflects Tanaka's status as both scholar and minister. Another work is Alfred Bloom's *A Life of Serendipity: Blown by the Wind of Amida's Vow.* Bloom is also an accomplished scholar and ordained Shin minister, but in this memoir he offers glimpses into his journey from the time of his youth, and as his religious journey unfolded organically from days long before he knew anything about Shin Buddhist philosophy. This kind of organic narrative helps to illuminate the religious quest as life process, one in which religious stories, personal reflections, and cultural observations are intertwined.

Jeff Wilson's *Buddhism of the Heart* similarly conveys his organic experience as he has found his way deeper into Shin Buddhism. Through a series of essays, vignettes, and stories, Jeff relates various life events, the contexts of his study and practice, along with personal reflections that are woven together into a colorful tapestry of thought, emotion, and experience. In his own words, "This book is about one of the ways in which people work to wake up to the true nature of life and of this universe we share—a universe that includes much suffering and much potential for going beyond suffering." Yet, this one way, Shin Buddhism, contains many ways. It includes reading works of Shin literature, attendance at the Sunday services of Shin Buddhist temples and its attendant liturgy of chanting, bowing—and even Buddhist dancing. There are Shin Dharma talks to be heard, retreats attended, and rich personal encounters with teachers. So too are there the myriad spontaneous life experiences framed in Shin terms, the comings and goings of people and things, and chance encounters where "sleeves brush past one another" that nevertheless carry great meaning. In *Buddhism from the Heart*, Jeff shares some of these intimate moments of joy and of suffering as when he meets with fellow seekers or when he describes the passing of close family members.

Through the discipline of a religious path, one comes to know more deeply oneself and others, and one gains greater command of one's life. At the same time, much of what we experience remains beyond our control, and so much of what we learn in life depends upon how we receive the circumstances of life and death beyond our grasp. As Jeff suggests, "Perhaps it would be helpful to think of Shin as a kind of artistic endeavor, an art of living with wisdom, humility, and gratitude through the heart that has been opened and the mind that has been filled with sacred stories, passed down, elaborated and reshaped generation after generation." Indeed, this is a helpful description of Shin Buddhism—for it is not a monastic path but welcomes all people, making no distinction between genders, social classes, educational backgrounds, wise or foolish. Jeff sums up the basic approach open to anyone seeking a religious path that is available to all: "In the Shin view awakening isn't something to strive desperately for and obtain through our own effort at study and meditation; it's something we settle into and receive."

This book, *Buddhism of the Heart*, is a welcome addition to the growing English-language literature on the vast tradition of Shin Buddhism.

Introduction:
Buddhism of the Heart

T HIS BOOK is about one of the ways in which people work to wake up to the true nature of life and of this universe we share—a universe that includes much suffering and much potential for going beyond suffering. It is about Buddhism, a very old and beautiful path, and particularly about Jodo Shinshu Buddhism, the most popular type of Buddhism in Japan and the oldest organized form of Buddhism in the West. Also known as Shin Buddhism, it belongs to the Pure Land tradition, the most widespread type of Buddhism today, especially in eastern Asia.

Shin Buddhism has a long history of scholarship and academic learning—but that won't be the focus of this book. Instead, I'm just going to talk about Buddhism in the manner that regular Pure Land Buddhists have always approached it: through story, anecdote, reflection—and humor. There are stories in this book that compare Shin and other Buddhisms, but their point is to show why *I* find value in practicing this form of Buddhism, not to suggest that you should, or that one Buddhism is really better than another. Rather, my goal is to convey a sense of how it *feels* to live as a Shin Buddhist, especially one in modern North America.

This seems important to me because whereas other Buddhisms often seem to be mainly about the mind, Jodo Shinshu is about the heart. It relies on emotions, imagination, and relationships between people to bring about spiritual awakening, an awakening that might be better described as the opening of the heart to "deep entrusting," rather than the enlightenment of the mind with penetrating wisdom. But this isn't to say that mind and heart are separate things.

Yet there is a greater degree of emphasis on "heart feeling" in Jodo Shinshu than in any of the many other forms of Buddhism I've encountered, and since this is crucial to how I approach my individual Buddhist life, that is where I want to put my focus in this book. As the Shin author Itsuki Hiroyuki wrote, "Religions do not originate in doctrines and organizations. They arise from natural human emotions." With that guidance in mind, this will be a collection of short essays designed to convey feelings and attitudes. I hope you will find some value in this approach. You can find some further reading suggestions in the back of this book for folks who want to explore doctrines, traditions, and history in greater depth, and you'll find a glossary back there too, since try as I may, you can't talk about Buddhism without using at least a few foreign terms.

One of the important things to understand about Shin is that for nearly 800 years it has been solely devoted to providing *laypeople* with a way in which to experience awakening and joy in their own everyday lives. And one of the primary methods that Jodo Shinshu hit upon was sacred storytelling. Through the written legends and oral traditions around Amida Buddha, the Pure Land, past saints and fools (who are often the same folks!), and present-day people, we encounter the transcendent elements of our mundane lives and begin to awaken to new, less self-centered ways of being. The life story of Shinran, the founder of Jodo Shinshu, is particularly important, but there are many others as well.

These sacred stories are a mixture of actual events and myth. It can be hard to tell these two elements apart—but fortunately telling them apart isn't the point. Our stories aren't important because they did or didn't happen exactly the way we tell them, but because they reveal aspects of how things are and how we can learn to live in accord with the Dharma, the reality that the Buddha uncovered. Lessons come in many forms and sometimes one story fits the occasion, sometimes another does. The truth of a story lies in the degree to which it points the hearer on toward deeper humility, awakening, and thankfulness. In fact, perhaps it would be helpful to think of Shin as a kind of artistic endeavor, an art of living with wonder, humility, and gratitude through the heart that has been opened and the mind that has been filled with sacred stories passed down, elaborated, and re-energized generation after generation.

In the Shin view, awakening isn't something we strive desperately for and obtain through our own efforts at study or meditation—it is something we settle into and receive. And it is through the stories and metaphors of the tradition and how they move us beyond the petty ego that we come closer to the entrusting heart, the heart that is rooted in gratitude and considerate awareness of others. When that entrusting heart glows within us we express our feelings by saying "Namu Amida Butsu," a joyful phrase called, in Japanese, the *nembutsu*. But don't mistake me here, please: the nembutsu is our *response* to awakening, not a *method* whereby we seek to awaken. Namu Amida Butsu is itself the final destination.

And before it comes the heart of trust and thankfulness. And before *that*, at the very beginning and at every step of the way, is the story.

Amida's Birth, Our Birth

Long ago—so long ago that we might say it was before the beginning of time as we know it—Amida became the buddha of boundless light and infinite life. These things, boundless light and infinite life, are, among other things, symbols of perfect wisdom and compassion. For eons before Amida became enlightened, this buddha-to-be was a bodhisattva named Dharma Storehouse, who spent his life accumulating enough merit that he would be able to share it with all living creatures and thus bring about the awakening of every single creature in the universe.

When Dharma Storehouse became Amida Buddha, the Pure Land of Ultimate Bliss sprang into being, powered by the force of the profound vows the bodhisattva made when he began his career. This Pure Land is the ultimate nature of reality, and stepping into that realm is entering nirvana and being freed of all suffering and delusion. Although we are all foolish, self-centered people, full of unwarranted pride and prone to harmful ways, Amida's boundless light embraces us all and never abandons us, no matter what we do.

It is always pursuing us, working to jolt us out of our egocentricity and wake us up to the wonder of this world that is ultimately "empty" of unchanging nature and yet minutely interconnected on every level.

When we finally stop relying on the leaky vessel of the false self and float instead on the warm ocean of Amida's compassion, we are liberated, just as we are, from the foibles of mortal existence. We are filled up with joy, and with a heart bursting with thankfulness, we proclaim our gratitude by saying "Namu Amida Butsu," intoning the name of that power beyond the ego-self which has opened us to true and real life. While our circumstances may be difficult, there is a touchstone of underlying peace and assurance that remains with us through the good and bad times, and when this life finishes and we leave our karmic attachments behind, we are welcomed fully into the Pure Land of Bliss.

This is the sacred story, recorded as a tale told by the Buddha in one of the first Mahayana Sutras, at the center of Pure Land Buddhism. It is a story of how we achieve our freedom and are awakened in this life, and how awakening is perfected when our life is over and we go beyond form and dualistic, ego-centered thinking. It is a promise of escape from our woes, of peace for our loved ones, and of reconciliation with strangers, enemies, and all forms of life. It is a restatement of the fundamental Buddhist truths in a mythopoetic form, one that puts in positive terms the things that the earliest Buddhist tradition described negatively, in terms of absence, such as "emptiness" and "extinction."

The Pure Land tradition goes back to India, to the earliest days of the Mahayana tradition, and it has spread from there to many parts of Asia and on to the West. Millions of people alive today experience their lives within the symbolic universe of this story, seeking to embody humility, trustingness, benevolence, simplicity, and pure happiness—even amid suffering.

This story has had a profound impact not only on the spiritual lives of such people, but also on the art, literature, politics, social structure, and many other aspects of Asian culture, especially in the eastern part of the continent. Far more than smaller monastic traditions like Zen or Tendai, it is the Pure Land tradition, shared by commoners and royalty alike, that has formed the basic Buddhist backbone of cultures like Japan and China for centuries.

It is amazing really, when you think about it.

A story, just a story, has so much power to move individual hearts and entire nations. It is just a tale told over and again, ancient and yet still alive today, continuing the work of liberation that the Buddha put into motion in ancient India. The story goes on and on, inviting new generations to take it up and discover its riches.

And every time someone hears the story and feels his or her heart respond with awe, Amida is born once more and the Pure Land is reopened to welcome home a long-wandering friend.

Amida's Nembutsu

THERE ARE many Shin temples in North America and Hawaii, as well as some in South America, Europe, and elsewhere— to say nothing of Japan, of course. Each is its own unique community of people, and Shin in different regions tends to be influenced by language, culture, and so on. But one thing you will find everywhere, regardless of where you go, is people saying the nembutsu: "Namu Amida Butsu." It may be a formal chant conducted during services, or a mumbling under the breath as one reflects on the Shin teachings. Yet however it is performed, the nembutsu is close to the heart of every Pure Land Buddhist.

This shared practice is what holds Shin practitioners together all over the world as a single body—it is said in the tradition that all people who say nembutsu are part of the same family. And in fact nembutsu is practiced in most forms of Buddhism, not just the officially Pure Land-based schools, so that is a large family indeed. The words are simple to understand—"Namu Amida Butsu" more or less translates as "I take refuge in Amida Buddha"—but there are many interpretations of what those words mean in relation to ourselves.

In Shin Buddhism, we don't think of nembutsu as a mantra, a prayer, or a formal practice designed to generate enlightenment. Shinran, the founder of Shin, had a deep understanding of human nature, an understanding that arose from awareness of his own limitations as a person bound by karmic circumstances beyond the possibility of full comprehension. He realized that any practice that strives for individual attainment, individual buddhahood—even practicing the nembutsu—is a possible avenue for further ego attachment. The problem is that we can begin to congratulate ourselves over how many times we've said nembutsu, or obsess over whether we should be saying it more, or feel pride that our chanting is so beautiful, and so on. Really, there are an infinite number of ways that the ego can spin traps, and spiritual practice is a fertile area for such foolishness. This applies not only to nembutsu but also to meditation, precepts, and virtually any aspect of religious life that we can imagine.

So instead, Shinran taught that we should think of nembutsu as the practice of Amida Buddha, not as our own. When we say nembutsu, we are allowing Amida's practice to flow through us. Nembutsu is therefore something in which we participate, not something that we produce—it is something we receive from beyond the ego-self. When we understand that our saying of the nembutsu is actually the call of reality itself reaching out to us, then there is nothing on which to base pride or shame. However many nembutsus we say or however we say them, they arise from beyond the self. This identification of Amida and nembutsu is so deep in the Shin tradition that I have even heard Shin ministers say that there is no Amida apart from the nembutsu.

Namu Amida Butsu.

Once Upon a Time

L ET ME TELL YOU a story about a great man who lived about 2,500 years ago. This man was born to a loving mother and father in a family of considerable power and wealth, who named him Siddhartha. His mother passed away soon after his birth, but his stepmother continued to care for him as if he were her own son. He grew up with all his needs taken care of: people fed him, clothed him, stimulated his mind, encouraged him to seek righteousness and truth (as they understood it, of course), and gave him lots of love. Eventually, a marriage was arranged for him to a beautiful and loving woman, and she bore him a son. As a member of the royal family, he existed literally on the work and generosity and love of the entire nation. Everything he had and was, he received from others.

As an adult, he wished to understand life beyond the simple fulfillment of his own desires. Venturing forth from the rarefied environment of palace life, he learned from the life of commoners the truths of old age, sickness, and death, and from a wandering holy man he learned of the age-old path of spiritual pursuit. Siddhartha's mind was opened to the suffering of other people, and suddenly all he could think of was his wish to end this suffering, for himself and all others. He left the palace, and was borne away by his faithful steed and horseman, till he crossed the Anoma River and left the world he knew behind.

For six years he wandered from place to place, learning from others. He learned how to fast, how to meditate, how to mortify the flesh. Siddhartha strove mightily to achieve his own enlightenment for himself, to understand the Self, which was the highest spiritual pursuit in ancient India and believed by many to be the path to release. Finally, as his body wasted away nearly to nothing and his efforts to quell suffering once and for all proved fruitless, he gave up his attachment to asceticism and the idea that his own efforts alone could free him.

Siddhartha went down to the stream and bathed. Its flowing waters cleansed and supported him, and as he bathed, a young outcaste girl offered him a meal. The food nourished and restored him, and with a mind of gratitude he walked through the forest. A young outcaste boy appeared and offered him fresh grass for a meditation seat, and sitting down beneath the sheltering branches of a tree, he relaxed back into an easy and natural state of reflection. Now that he had stopped trying to win enlightenment through his own extreme effort, his mind was clear and he began to see into the nature of all things.

He saw how in innumerable past existences he had traveled toward this moment, supported by the work and kindness of others, and learned to perfect the virtues by helping them in turn. He saw into the emptiness of all things, their interdependent and mutual co-arising, and saw that there was in fact no essential Self after all. A rainstorm arose, and the giant Serpent King spread his cobra's hood to protect the seated man. The evil god Mara appeared to frighten and tempt Siddhartha. When this failed, he challenged the young man's right to liberation. Siddhartha simply bent and touched the earth with his hand. Mother Earth trembled and sprang up, wringing the ocean from her hair and washing Mara away. Siddhartha sat serenely, his eye on the rising morning star, and he came ever after to be known as the Buddha, the One Who Awakened.

The Buddha became the Buddha because of his father and mother, because of his courtiers and the peasants in the fields, because of the horse that he rode to the forest, the sages who encouraged his pursuits, the ascetics who taught him mortification and also ultimately let him see that mortification isn't the answer, the stream that bathed him, the girl who fed him and the food, the boy and the grass, the tree, the Serpent King, and the earth, because of the star that rose and shone just-as-it-was, because of the air that Siddhartha breathed in as he sat, because of the sun that provided him heat and nourished the plants he ate—everything everywhere came together to produce the Buddha. And most of all, the Buddha became the Buddha because he was already held by the liberated nature of reality to begin with—he only discovered what had been the true state of himself and all things, all beings all along: vast emptiness, nothing set aside and holy, nothing outside of the inter-connected embrace of reality.

The Buddha did not discover something unique and special about himself. He did not become something different from other things or people. He awakened to the true nature of all things (him-self included) as liberated *suchness*. This awakening came after he had been supported in innumerable ways by countless beings and conditions, and after he had ceased to strive after enlightenment and relaxed back into his natural state. As a much later Japanese

Zen thinker named Dogen said, "To study the Buddha way is to study the self. To study the self is to forget the 'self.' To forget the 'self' is to be enlightened by all things."

I'm not saying that the Buddha put out no effort. But effort too is empty of independent-nature and arises interdependently from the contingency of all things. Siddhartha could only put out "his" effort after and while being supported by the entire universe. Likewise, our own efforts toward deeper insight and understanding can only take place within an infinite matrix of supportive actions by others.

How lucky we are to live in such an open-ended universe, where we can receive what we need from others and contribute toward the happiness and awakening of one another.

Strawberries

WHEN WE LIVED in North Carolina, my wife and I went strawberry-picking one spring morning and brought home more than our little household could manage. So we got busy making strawberry pies, strawberry ice cream, strawberry preserves, etc. It was a nice way to pass the weekend, and the result was that we had gifts to give to friends and co-workers.

Spending a couple of hours out in the sun, working the rows of berries in the field, got me thinking about our relationship with the earth. It reminded me of a passage I had recently read in Taigen Dan Leighton's book, *Faces of Compassion:*

> The image of Shakyamuni touching the ground, and the emergence of the Earth Goddess as witness, reveal the quality of Buddhism as an earth religion. This is a central fact of bodhisattva practice. Everything we need for awakening is present in the very ground upon which we sit. Enlightenment is not a matter of achieving some brand-new state of

being or consciousness, or of traveling to some distant realm, or of becoming some new, different person. Rather, the transformation embodied in Shakyamuni's awakening is simply about fully settling into the deep, wide self we already are, totally interconnected with the whole universe, but expressed uniquely in this individual life. This experience is as close to us as the ground beneath our feet. It is not achieved in some other, external, heavenly realm. The earth we sit on is rich and fertile, teeming with life and awareness.

In Shin Buddhism, we have a type of person called a myokonin. Basically, these are just regular people—often totally uneducated—who express their awakening through the ordinary activities of their lives. Tales of these famous laypeople, usually collected from oral folklore, are an important part of our tradition. One famous myokonin, Saichi, said something similar to Leighton, though in fewer words:

> O Saichi, where is your Land of Bliss?
> My Land of Bliss is right here.
> Where is the line of division
> between this world and the Land of Bliss?
> The eye is the line of division.

This is a crucial teaching to reflect on. The division between us and the Land of Bliss is not the line between life and death. It is not the line between the good and the bad. It is the eye/I that creates the division.

When the eye sees clearly, the Pure Land is perceived right here and now, in the warmth of the sun, the richness of the soil, the taste of strawberries.

Appreciating the Furniture

IN OUR NORMAL, unenlightened experience, we go through life as if stumbling around in a dark room. We bump into the table and cry out, "Stupid thing! Who put that there?" We knock over the lamp: "Argh! Somebody should've bolted that down!" Flailing about, we crash into the ottoman. "What an idiotic place for a footstool!"

Unawakened, we continually encounter unseen difficulties, and compounding our problems, when we encounter such difficulties we curse and blame all those things on others.

Yet all we need to do in order to remedy this tragicomic situation is… turn on a light. Once a light has been turned on, we can avoid bumping into the table, lamp, or footstool. The furniture doesn't go away, of course, just as illumination in this life does not eradicate our humanity and foolish passions. Aided by the light, we navigate through our lives more smoothly, and feel thankful that we are out of the dark.

This is a story that I have heard Dr. Taitetsu Unno use to show

how when we awaken to Amida's grasp, nothing really changes—the furniture (our karmic limitations of greedy attachment, hostility, and self-centered delusion) is all still in place, but we are no longer threatened by it or curse it. He calls this "understanding that this life is a good life." This life becomes a good life when we realize that it is a good life, that we are given all that we need and that we are never abandoned by great compassion and wisdom.

Yet there is a further point about all this that occurs to me: the furniture doesn't become just relatively harmless when we receive this illumination—it actually becomes *useful*. In the light, we can see to use the table to eat at, read beneath the lamp, rest our feet on the stool. Discovering that this life is a good life means waking up to the truth that both our difficulties and our gifts are opportunities, that even our deep karmic limitations are great teachers for understanding reality and experiencing the joy of liberation.

The truth is that as long as we live, we will never be fully rid of our natural passions. Not only will we fail to eradicate them, but we need some of them to survive!

Shinran, the founder of Shin Buddhism, had this insight, and it was a radical break from the sagely path of other Buddhists of his day. He saw this truth in the hard everyday realities of the fishermen and peasants with whom he lived in exile because of religious persecution. The passions of our lives are not simply devils lurking with minds eager for sin—when we are shown them in the light of wisdom we realize that they too are part of the great Vow that supports and sustains our lives. We can say thank you to the shadows that make us appreciate the light that much more, and learn to use all our gifts appropriately and in the spirit of gratitude.

Inner Togetherness

W HEN EUROPEANS first encountered Buddhism, they
believed it was a negativistic, nihilistic faith. This was
based on a misunderstanding of the true meaning of the
Buddha's insight into the vital issue of suffering, and the poorly
understood concept of *shunyata,* emptiness, which they thought
meant "nothingness." What's more, they were horrified by a religion that doesn't give credence to the idea of God or the individual
soul. While Westerners' understanding of Buddhism has generally
become more sophisticated, these original misconceptions still
haunt many people's ideas about the Dharma. How can a religion
whose core realization is "emptiness" possibly be anything other
than nihilistic?

This concept of *shunyata* is linked historically to the Indian
monk Nagarjuna, who is considered the first of the seven great Pure
Land masters of the past by Shin Buddhism. The point Nagarjuna
was making about *shunyata* was that all things arise interdependently, thus they are empty of self-nature. I can remember what an

impact it had on me years ago when I encountered the Vietnamese Buddhist monk Thich Nhat Hanh's translation of *shunyata* as "interbeing." When emptiness is seen as inter-relatedness, as in the concept of interbeing, it can become more approachable. It avoids the sort of traps that ideas of nothingness tend to include. Here was the key I needed to really move affirmatively into Buddhism.

I had a similar moment of insight and appreciation when encountering the work of the Shin scholar Kaneko Daiei, who speaks of the idea of "inner togetherness" in his essay "The Meaning of Salvation in the Doctrine of Pure Land Buddhism":

> One thing should be remembered in connection with the problem of suffering: every one of us human beings is deeply interrelated with fellow beings in an inner togetherness. It can hardly be doubted that we are so born as to be sensitive of our inner togetherness. Do we not implicitly mean this when we use the term 'we'? In this sense, our inner togetherness may be called 'we-ness.' As long as our fellow beings are unhappy, none of us can remain aloof from them. We cannot but share the unhappiness with them. Because of the inner togetherness of man, sympathy can be awakened within us.

For Kaneko, togetherness is the fulfillment of the bodhisattva ideal, which strives to create an awareness of co-identity between beings so that they will assist each other in the universal work of liberation.

As I understand it, *togetherness* also functions as a synonym for *shunyata:* emptiness as the togetherness of all things co-arising simultaneously, all dependent on one another. This togetherness is realized in *shinjin,* the trusting heart, when we see that we are all mutually embraced by Amida. And from this rises the grounds for

Pure Land activism in the world: seeing the equality of self and other and realizing that our opponents suffer from the same afflictions which we do.

When we see this, we can put aside egoism and work to create the conditions for peace.

Co-living

Togetherness IS PERHAPS the one word that moves me most about the Pure Land tradition. It is expressed in the canonical stories as the desire to be born together with all beings—people, bugs, critters, whales, and so on—in Amida's realm. We don't just seek our own salvation—we are only fully happy when we can be born together with all others. No one is left behind by Amida, no one is left out. This does not sound like the sort of society that we live in today, but it does give us something to aspire for. One of Amida's vows is that all people in the Land of Bliss will have an appearance of gold—that is, that regardless of what we look like, we will all be highly valued. This togetherness has a technical term in Pure Land Buddhism: *kyosei*, which translates as "co-living" or "symbiosis."

Specifically, kyosei is the application of "born together with all beings" to our present, imperfect world. I don't believe that this difficult, stressful world of ours can ever fully become a Pure Land in the sense that it will be free of all problems. Yet even so the Pure

Land is never apart from this world, and we have the ability to work to alleviate more of the world's suffering. Thankful for the blessings we receive, we can try to be kinder, more open-minded, and more accepting of one another. And we can work to eliminate barriers between people, so that our togetherness is brought to light and honored.

During my time in Japan I encountered something that seemed to drive home the fundamental heart-feeling of togetherness in Pure Land Buddhism. Chionji is a temple in northeastern Kyoto, belonging to the Jodo Shu school, which was founded by Shinran's teacher, Honen. The temple has a very unusual artifact: the largest Buddhist rosary *(nenju)* in the world. The nenju is made out of large wooden beads about the size of a person's fist, strung together in a string so long it loops around and around the inside of the large worship hall. But the nenju is more than just an incredible artifact—it is also a practice. On the fifteenth of every month, laypeople and priests come together to collectively chant one million nembutsu while holding the nenju as a group.

I was very stirred by this giant nenju and the million-nembutsu practice, because to me it expresses the deep feeling of Pure Land Buddhism. Everyone, monk and lay, gathers with one another and holds on to the nenju—thus they are all equal and connected. The nenju is a huge circle, so there is no beginning or end to the nembutsu and the people who embody it, and no one higher or lower. Although they each have an individual encounter with the Buddha, they are expressing a wish to be born together. Thus even as they sort out their own awakening, they acknowledge the importance of the community and the relationships that they hold dear. This seems like togetherness given concrete form, in a commonly held nenju, in a shared nembutsu chant and in hearts beating as one in the wish to embody and express our fundamental togetherness.

Offering Incense

WHEN I LIVED in Los Angeles, I would sometimes attend Sunday services at the Nishi Hongwanji Los Angeles Betsuin, the main Shin headquarters for Southern California. This is a very large temple in the Jodo Shinshu tradition, more than a hundred years old and with three full-time ministers. During the sutra-chanting, everyone filed up one by one to bow before the Buddha and offer incense. And afterward, people came up as representatives of various temple organizations to also offer incense. Because the temple has such an active life, it took quite a long while as the facilitator called out one group after another: "Cub scouts, boy scouts, girl scouts, Dharma School, Young Buddhists' Association, Men's Association, Fujinkai…"

People sometimes assume that chanting is the center of Pure Land practice. But it has always seemed to me that the service, whether conducted at home or in the temple, culminates in the incense-offering. In a way, this simple act is more important than the nembutsu, sutra-chanting, community announcements, even the Dharma talk. In the act of offering incense—approaching the altar, giving a pinch of powdered incense, bowing with palms together, saying the nembutsu, and departing—the inner feeling of Buddhism is expressed. It is in this moment that we come face to face with the Buddha, when "Namu (myself) meets Amida Butsu (true reality)," as we say in the Shin tradition.

The guest speaker one morning at the Betsuin was Reverend Mas Kodani, minister of the Senshin Buddhist Temple. After watching everyone piously offering incense, he was ready to knock us all down a peg or two. He delivered a very humorous Dharma talk about how people always check to make sure their hair is in place and their clothes look right before they approach the altar, and how once they get there they put on a show of looking very humble and proper. All of this is foolish ego, he reminded us, and is precisely beside the point. When offering incense, the right attitude is not "how do I look" or "I sure am humble," but simply to offer incense and meet the Buddha without an extra thought.

After chastising everyone (including himself—at length), Reverend Kodani offered a story of true entrusting. He reminded everyone of an incident that happened in the temple decades ago, but that some people might still remember: A service was being held, and a little old granny got up to offer incense. She was all bent over and walked so slow. Tiny step by step she approached the incense burner—it must've taken her five minutes to get there! When she got to the burner, she dropped in a pinch of incense and bent her head. Her nembutsu was so soft no one could hear it over the chanting, but everyone was deeply moved. This was real. She was just offering incense, just saying the nembutsu, just encountering true reality moment by moment. Then she took a long, long time making her way back to her seat again.

Reverend Kodani recommended such an attitude to us at all

times, and I do try to live this as much as I can. Every act can be one of offering and of encountering the Buddha. But I still have a special fondness for the incense offering and bow. Even if we are phony during the rest of the day, at that moment we are forced to confront who we are and how we are operating. If we are phony before the Buddha, we will be awakened to this fact. And if we are genuine before the Buddha, then our offering, bow, and nembutsu truly touches the heart of reality.

Mindfulness of the
Land of Bliss

I WAS THINKING RECENTLY of an important passage in the famous scripture known as the *Contemplation of Amida Sutra.* According to the story, this sutra was preached to Queen Vaidehi by Shakyamuni Buddha after she was imprisoned by her wicked son Ajatasatru. It is thus significant because it is directed to someone who is (1) a layperson, (2) a woman, and (3) an imprisoned criminal (she had committed the crime of high treason by helping her imprisoned husband survive). It is therefore a teaching expressly directed at the sort of people who were often left out of the elite male monastic traditions that have dominated much of Buddhism.

The passage upon which I was reflecting is this:

The Buddha said to Ananda and Vaidehi, "After you have contemplated thus, next visualize yourself as born in the Western Land of Utmost Bliss sitting cross-legged upon a lotus-flower. Visualize this lotus-flower as closed; as it opens, five hundred rays of colored light illuminate your body; then your eyes are open and you see buddhas and bodhisattvas filling the sky and hear the sounds of water, birds, and trees, and the voices of the buddhas all expounding the wonderful Dharma in accord with the twelve divisions of the scriptures. When you rise from meditation, keep those things in mind and do not forget them. Seeing them thus is called the visualization of the Land of Utmost Bliss of the Buddha Amida. This is the comprehensive visualization, and is known as the twelfth contemplation.

"Innumerable transformed bodies of Amida, together with those of Avalokiteshvara and Mahasthamaprapta, will always accompany those who contemplate thus."

Obviously, this is a beautiful passage and significant because it poetically describes the process of awakening as one is born into the Pure Land. But I wanted to discuss it here because of a more subtle teaching.

Notice that Shakyamuni says that this isn't just about contemplating our future fate when we attain the Pure Land and are released into full nirvana after death—he says that when we are finished with the formal visualization we should keep this mindfulness and not forget these things. This means that we should view this world through the lens of the Pure Land during our life, and specifically we should look upon the clouds and stars of the air as innumerable buddhas and bodhisattvas, and recognize the sounds of babbling brooks, singing birds, and wind whispering in the trees as the true sounds of Dharma.

This is an ancient Buddhist method for recognizing the sacred nature of this world apart from our mistaken experience of it as samsara, and with these environmental triggers we can always try to maintain mindfulness and see that the Dharma is naturally being expressed by all things.

All we need to do is let everything that is not our own self-centered calculations freely express this inherent Dharma to us.

Fear of Falling

WHEN I GRADUATED COLLEGE and moved to New York City, I had an interest in Buddhism, especially Zen. I spent years doing intense investigation into many forms of Buddhism and spending many hours in painful cross-legged meditation. By the time I left New York for North Carolina in 2001, I'd committed to the Jodo Shinshu tradition of Pure Land Buddhism. Particularly appealing to me was its emphasis on sincerity, humility, naturalness, and gratitude as the keys to living an authentic life.

Leaving New York was the right decision for me—it felt good to give up on the crowding, the commutes, the expense, and the other problems of the concrete jungle—but there are no Jodo Shinshu temples in North Carolina. So, once a month, I was forced to return to my home temple in New York to connect with my community of fellow practitioners and participate in a training program for lay teachers. The only problem is that to get there, I had to fly.

There's something profoundly counterintuitive about climbing aboard a 400-ton metal contraption loaded with 50,000 gallons of highly flammable fuel in order to fly several miles up into the thin air. Especially when the nightly news regularly feeds us spectacular images of planes blowing up or falling out of the sky like meteors, often for no greater reason than faulty wiring or an unfortunate encounter with a seagull.

When you're risking your life in the face of fiery death 30,000 feet above sea level, you focus on the essentials. *Why am I doing this?* I'd ask myself. *What do I hope to accomplish? How did I get from being an agnostic science major to a vegetarian Buddhist chanting my way across America? What is it about Pure Land Buddhism that leads me to step onto this deathtrap?*

The answers that arose for me all related to the place of gratitude in the Pure Land tradition. This focus on gratitude toward all as essential to our awakening, and the ideal of equality of all beings without distinction, were powerful parts of Jodo Shinshu's appeal for me. Shin seemed to lack what sometimes looked like the spiritual arrogance or self-centeredness I've encountered at times in other Buddhist traditions. Too often, it seemed to me, people harbor some kind of misplaced pride—in their ability to adhere to codes of morality, or to attain special and unusual states of mind, or because they'd received the most powerful initiations from the most famous gurus or teachers. After years of practice in Zen I found these very attitudes developing within myself. But in Jodo Shinshu there are no spiritual elites, just fellow practitioners, all equal in the embrace of Amida's compassion and wisdom. And chanting nembutsu is an activity available to all people in any situation, not just those who can afford the time to sit on a cushion for hours on end or pay for expensive retreats. As a young person without much time or money to spend on Dharma, these were important distinctions.

Whenever I fly, I say the nembutsu quietly under my breath. But nembutsu isn't a type of prayer—ideally it's supposed to be a statement of thanksgiving. But I have to admit for me in the air it can be more a sort of desperate distraction. *Namu-Amida-Butsu, Namu-Amida-Butsu—oh god what was that sound?!?—Namu-Amida-Butsu, Namu-Amida-Butsu, Namu-Amida-Butsu—I really hope they sell alcohol on this flight—Namu-Amida-Butsu...*

There's a famous passage in the *Tannisho*, a basic scripture of Jodo Shinshu, in which Shinran addresses pilgrims who have braved a war-torn countryside to reach him: "Each of you has come to see me, crossing the borders of more than ten provinces at the risk of your life, solely with the intent of asking about the path to birth in the land of bliss." This passage replays in my head whenever I go to the airport. I steel myself to travel hundreds of miles through the freezing atmosphere, helpless before the power of weather, mechanics, and all the rest, in order to listen to the Dharma. Every time the pilot turns on the seatbelt light, I realize that, against all odds, I have found a sort of faith.

Pure Land Buddhism teaches that the source of our suffering is clinging to egocentricity and the deluded belief that one's own individual power is itself fully sufficient to overcome the deep resentment, greed, and ignorance that mark human life. We are counseled to rely wholly on Other Power, the natural activity of all things to reveal our inner togetherness with all things. Flying plays right into this in a nastily direct way: Unless you're the pilot, flying is a complete surrender, which is why so many folks prefer to drive even though it's a far more dangerous manner of travel. Truly giving up self-power is virtually impossible, especially for many Americans. But on a plane you have to relinquish that power—relinquish it, or go crazy.

But even on the ground, our ideas of power and control are really illusions.

I went back to reading about Shinran's address to the pilgrims from far provinces: "If you imagine in me some special knowledge of a path to birth other than the nembutsu or of scriptural writings that teach it, you are greatly mistaken." In other words, to these travelers who risked everything to meet him and listen to the deepest truth of life, Shinran said that the nembutsu was enough. All they had to do was give up their self-attachment and everything would work out. It sounds so easy, but I've learned that it's a wrenching requirement to fulfill.

We have to just let whatever comes come, be it pleasure or fear—and let whatever goes go.

"Please discontinue the use of all portable electronic devices"—*Namu-Amida-Butsu*. "Your seat cushion also acts as a flotation device"—*Namu-Amida-Butsu*. "Please return to your seat and stow your tray table to an upright and locked position"—*Namu-Amida-Butsu*.

Although it's the most difficult of all difficulties, acceptance is the only real option. And so I keep flying and keep entrusting myself to Other Power, come what may.

Trusting the Dharma

RECENTLY, I WAS PONDERING what it is exactly in which Pure Land Buddhists put their trust. Often, you read descriptions by outsiders about how we place our faith in a particular Buddha, Amida, which leads some to imagine that Pure Land is almost a sort of Christian Buddhism. But when I reflect on it, I feel that actually we place our trust in the Dharma. Rather than desperately trying to bring about our own buddhahood, we recognize that if we relax and don't stick our foolish egos in the way of things, then the Dharma will naturally bring about our transformation. I don't mean to diminish the role of Amida Buddha here. But it seems to me that Amida is the means by which the Dharma, the truth of things-as-they-are, acts upon us to help us awaken to liberation.

Dharma isn't a person, it isn't a being to be supplicated to. It's just the way things work, the reality of the universe unfolding as a process in time. The Buddha discovered and taught about a portion of this universe, and science can reveal a portion too, as can any contemplation or activity that accords with the way things actually are. Part of this fact of existence is that our egocentricity brings about endless problems. But another fact is that when we learn to give up on ego-centeredness and allow reality to unfold without our muddling, it works effortlessly to bring us to awakening. This is deep trust in the Dharma.

The modern Shin teacher Nobuo Haneda, in the introduction to one of his books, says:

> Shakyamuni's experience of enlightenment may be likened to a jagged rock pounded by violent waves. As long as the rock is jagged, the incessantly pounding waves inevitably produce turbulence as they wash over its rough edges. But once the waves have worn down the rock, making it smooth and round, the turbulence ceases. Likewise, when a person loses his rigidness of self through the challenge of the Dharma, he becomes selfless. Selflessness is humility. Since the self is the cause of unfreedom, its loss leads to freedom. In this sense, humility and freedom go hand in hand. Only a humble person can be free. Buddhism is a path leading to humility and freedom.

I like this image of the self as a jagged rock gradually worn down by the pounding waves, and Haneda's emphasis on humility, a core value for Shin Buddhists. With humility as a value, we don't have to pretend that we are something other than what we truly are.

Really, we never gain anything by hiding who we are. So many times I have met others who are putting on a face of spirituality, but are really hiding jagged rocks. I too have been guilty of this too many times to count. If we ignore those jagged rocks and try to pretend they aren't there, for a time the waves may flow over us more smoothly. But really we are not getting any better or making any advancement on the Dharma path. Ultimately, we are just delaying our development by pretending to be more selfless than we really are, and setting ourselves up for disaster when we finally come crashing helplessly into the rocks of self.

It's common to fear exposing our faults, so we may wear a mask of false-selflessness. But what we need to do is develop trust in the embracing ocean of the Dharma. Hiding oneself is ultimately a crisis of faith, an action that says "I don't really trust that things will be alright unless I pretend to be something I'm not." But Amida accepts us just as we are. If we have confidence that the process of Dharma will work out our liberation naturally, we can let go of the mask and let ourselves be worn down through the working of Other Power, which is the active expression of Dharma.

A Universe of White Ashes

THERE ARE MANY FAMOUS WRITINGS in Jodo Shinshu Buddhism, but among them there are a few that we return to time and again throughout our lives. One of these is Rennyo's letter on white ashes, in his collection *Gobunsho*. Rennyo was a descendant of Shinran and a great reformer of the Shin tradition. Many of the practices that we perform derive from Rennyo, such as chanting Shinran's song of true entrusting, the *Shoshinge*. In the letter on white ashes, Rennyo tells his followers:

When I deeply contemplate the transient nature of human existence, I realize that, from beginning to end, life is impermanent like an illusion. We have not yet heard of anyone who lived ten thousand years. How fleeting is a lifetime!

Who in this world today can maintain a human form for even a hundred years? There is no knowing whether I will die first or others, whether death will occur today or tomorrow.

We depart one after another more quickly than the dew-drops on the roots or the tips of the blades of grasses.

I remember thinking this was rather depressing the first time I read it, but over the years it has slowly unfolded for me as it came to have ever more relevance and meaning in my life. One way that we can identify the enduring Shin classics is in how they continue to provide us with fresh insights even when we were sure we had already thoroughly understood them. So it is with the chapter on white ashes, which hides amazing depths in its short few sentences.

Normally, White Ashes is read as a meditation on our own mortality and impermanence, as suggested by the use of the pronoun "we" when rendering it into English. "In the morning we may have rosy cheeks; in the evening we may become white ashes." "We" is inclusive and suggests that the reader is to imagine him or herself becoming white ashes by the end of the day. Therefore, we conclude, you should not take your life lightly, but live in gratitude and say the nembutsu. This is how I always understood it—until recently.

My son was born at the beginning of 2007, and as it turned out, the delivery was extremely difficult. My wife was severely injured and faced death, and though the baby seemed all right, it was impossible to tell if there might be something wrong with him resulting from the difficult labor. Things were about as dire as they could possibly be. I remember at one point in the middle of the night my mother-in-law pleading with the doctors, "Please, don't let her die!" What was supposed to be the best day of our lives was turning into the very worst.

On the second day, I was sick of the hospital food and felt that I wanted to get outside for a little while. So I walked down the street and ate in a Thai restaurant. After about forty-five minutes, I started back to the hospital. As I walked, I thought about how I didn't know what was going on back in the intensive care unit. It was quite possible that while I was out, my wife or son or both had, in just these few minutes, passed away. Although I was in good health and had just had a tasty meal, circumstances might have already occurred that would ensure that in a few moments I would be miserable. The rosy cheeks of my wife or baby might already be white as ash.

It was then that I realized that Rennyo's message has two sides. It isn't enough to realize our own mortality and try to live thankfully for the time we have. We also have to be aware of the brutally impermanent nature of everything we love, and live in such a way that we never take them for granted. Truly, I think it would be easier for me to die in peace than it would be to go on living after the death of my loved ones. But regardless of my feelings, everyone I care for will disappear eventually.

Now I wonder if this wasn't an even more important point for Rennyo, who lived a long life while watching wife after wife and child after child die. As a person of *shinjin*, the trusting heart, Rennyo knew that if he was white ashes in the evening it would merely mean he had returned to his natural home in the Pure Land. But as the survivor of so much loss, he was deeply aware that those left behind are the ones who bear the full burden of mortality.

I did not quicken my pace as these thoughts came to me. If my wife and son had already passed, what could I do? Instead, I just chanted nembutsu softly as I walked along Wilshire Boulevard back toward the hospital. For the years my wife had given me and the hours received from my son, I was grateful. Although of course I would be devasted to discover either of them no longer alive, in any case, I would strive to be grateful now and each day forward, or else lose the chance to show them how much they meant to me.

Mother and baby are fine now and we are all happy. But White Ashes has changed for me. Now when I read it I am reminded not only of my own mortality but of that of others as well, and I realize that truly we live in a universe of white ashes, where everything is already on its way to destruction. I can do nothing to stop this. But today, right now, my wife, baby, and I have rosy cheeks, and I can say the nembutsu in joy and gratitude not only for the time I am allowed with them, but also the time they are allowed with me.

Charmless

URING ONE of my research trips in Japan, I was struck by some of the ways that Jodo Shinshu is different from less popular forms of Japanese Buddhism. I visited many temples of various sects and observed the practices they promote. Especially interesting to me were the charms, amulets, and oracles that seem to be the basic stock-and-trade of Nichiren, Shingon, and Zen—every Buddhist sect, in fact, except Jodo Shinshu. In every country Buddhism has made some accommodation with the mundane wishes of everyday life, providing some sort of magic to influence the cosmic forces of luck and fortune. But even though it was founded to minister to laypeople, Jodo Shinshu alone seems to avoid that approach.

The difference was brought home to me most forcefully in a Buddhist cemetery. Perhaps this is significant, since the graveyard is the central realm of Buddhist practice in Japan, maybe even more than the worship hall. As I wandered through a Jodo Shinshu cemetery, I mused on the fact that while the graveyard was large, most of the graves themselves were very similar. There were no statues of bodhisattvas or buddhas and no *toba*—the tall wooden plaques found in most Japanese graveyards. Then, in a distant corner of graveyard, I saw a bunch of toba sticking up. I hurried over, but when I got there, I found a low wall in the way. I was looking over it into another cemetery next to it, belonging to a separate temple. As it turned out, the other temple was not Jodo Shinshu, but Jodo Shu, a related form of Pure Land Buddhism that nonetheless has some significant differences. That other cemetery was full of various bodhisattvas, buddhas, and deities, with toba of all sizes and charms hanging off many gravestones.

Jodo Shu and Jodo Shinshu are often thought of as very close to one another. Certainly, of all the types of Buddhism, none is more similar to Shin than Jodo Shu, and they are our companions in nembutsu. So I think it really says something that the contrast between these two adjoining cemeteries was so stark. On the Jodo Shu side, many different Buddhist saviors were being pleaded to for salvation, toba were being made to send merit to help out people in the afterlife, and sundry mantras and other practices were being invoked. Meanwhile, the Jodo Shinshu graveyard simply held memorials for the dead, so that the living could remember them and have some solace. A Shin cemetery was totally unlike any other Japanese Buddhist graveyard I'd been in.

It is natural for us to want the comfort of magic and charms. Life is a challenge and sometimes the promise of any kind of help is heartening. We are privileged to have something much more special, something exceptional in Japan and indeed in Buddhism: assurance of liberation through Other Power, which never abandons us. Whether we buy charms or not, whether we rely on one Buddha or a hundred, whether we are good or bad, it makes no difference. Our ultimate awakening is settled, and so is that of our loved ones—end of story.

In fact, even all those nervous people in other Buddhisms—and other religions—will also be inevitably grasped by Other Power as well. Eight hundred years after Shinran, such a realization remains revolutionary in Japanese Buddhism, and in human religion generally. Abandoning fear and anxiety about this world and the next, we can appreciate what a gift we have been given and return our thanks in gratitude with nembutsu and acts of loving-kindness.

Playing in Someone Else's Backyard

AS A PROFESSOR and Shin lay teacher, I've been called upon to speak in all sorts of venues. One of the more unusual ones was the adult Vacation Bible School class at the North Raleigh Presbyterian Church. I was invited to give an introductory talk on Buddhism to these curious Christians. I didn't quite know what to expect going in, but I ended up having a good time. These were inquisitive, open-minded folks who asked some excellent questions.

Although I was called in to speak as the expert, I ended up receiving an unexpected lesson myself. While we were chatting, we discovered that the pastor of the North Raleigh church served my late grandmother's church before I came to live with her, and used to visit her regularly at our house. This lady had been very nice to my grandmother and still thought of her warmly. I was taken by surprise to discover this relationship with a stranger from a different town and separate religion. Reverend Taitetsu Unno once told me at the New York Buddhist Church that in Japan there's a saying about how even the momentary brushing of two strangers' sleeves in the marketplace is rooted in ancient, unknowable karma.

I felt like I was suddenly confronted with this fact when this stranger, who'd contacted me serendipitously via my graduate school, described spending hours sitting in my kitchen listening to my grandmother—just as I had done. No matter how well we think we know ourselves, our family, our town, and all the things that interact in our life, there is always a larger, more complex web of circumstance that we can never hope to fully perceive. Contrary to the usual Buddhist hope of obtaining ultimate knowledge and being able to discern all the interconnections that produce the world, the universe is actually more mysterious, fascinating, and brain-bursting than we can possibly handle.

I'd come to the church to teach them about Buddhism, but I ended up learning a lesson about reality from them. Even if inter-faith dialogue is difficult because of the alternate ways in which we conceive and talk about religion, ultimately we are all trying our best to understand truths that go beyond conceptions and words.

And yet, even in the midst of frustrations over language, we can achieve deeper insight by remaining open to the experiences and lessons of people with other approaches to Buddhism, or other religions altogether.

I'm grateful to that Christian pastor and her congregation for helping me realize this.

Buddha-Nature,
Scorpion-Nature

I N JAPAN there are many novels with a Buddhist aspect to them, but few are available to the average English reader. One that I especially enjoyed was *The Buddha Tree*. It was written in 1966 by Niwa Fumio, who was a priest in the Takada branch of Shin Buddhism.

Because of my studies, I rarely have the opportunity to read fiction anymore, but I was able to justify *The Buddha Tree* to myself since it deals with Japanese Buddhism. And I'm glad I did.

The heart of the book is about how the priest is caught in a web of human weakness and deception, despite his desire to be good and truthful. Niwa really captures the impossibilities and tragedies of real life, the truth that no matter how hard we strive to be wholly good, we always fall short of the mark. This is true for people in the temple as well as out in the world. Without being preachy, Niwa breathes life (via his modern characters) into Shinran's existential discovery about our inability to control our lives and even ourselves, and the ever-present wisdom and compassion that nonetheless enfolds us.

I'm not sure that I can claim that all my years of involvement with Buddhism have made me a better person. What I'm most aware of, in fact, is just how less than perfect I am. It is Buddhism that has woken me up to my imperfections and given me the ability to chuckle at my needy little ego's constant attempts to find security and self-aggrandizement in an ever-shifting, largely indifferent world. I can't really hope to keep the precepts, as much as I sincerely wish to do so. I can't even manage to perform my service before the home altar regularly.

I guess there is one advantage to realizing that you're never going to get it right: you do begin to stop expecting everyone else to get it right too, which makes for less frustration when other people turn out to be just as human as you are.

Another piece of Japanese literature that I justified reading because of its Buddhist aspect was Miyazawa Kenji's *Milky Way Railroad,* a famous Japanese children's story. There's an interesting passage where the train is flying past the constellation Scorpio, and someone tells a story about the meaning of the celestial critter.

According to the storyteller, Scorpio used to be a regular old scorpion, scuttling around, killing and eating many bugs and other creepy-crawlies. Then one day a weasel tried to eat him. The scorpion ran away, but was so frantic to escape that he fell into a deep well that he couldn't climb out of. As he lay at the bottom of the well, the scorpion reflected on his life and decided that his death was a waste. All these years he had killed other beings, but when his own life was in danger, he fled in fear and would now die without being of benefit to anyone. If the weasel had eaten him, at least the scorpion's body would have nourished another living being. The scorpion prayed that in future lives he would be able to selflessly sacrifice himself to help others, including those who sought to harm him, even if it meant suffering and dying for their sake.

Because of his prayer, he was transported into the heavens, where his body—transformed into stars—shone to light the way of the lost and confused.

Hard-Assed and Sore-Throated Buddhists

ONCE GAVE an unforgivably rambling presentation about Pure Land Buddhism to some very patient Zen folks in North Carolina. When I described the experience to a friend, he imagined a scene of me telling a bunch of Zennists that all their meditation is just giving them hardened asses. I had to chuckle at that one, both because it's a funny image and because it's really not the sort of thing I would say. But he was getting at a very serious issue: what is the place of meditation in Buddhism? And even more to the point, what is the place of the mind of awakening? For me, there's a lot of overlap between these two issues.

I grew up Unitarian-Universalist, which means I was taught self-reliance as a religious virtue and told to eschew dependence on supernatural saviors. Therefore I pretty much had to exhaust self-power attempts before I could open up to the possibility of Other Power, which I persisted in misunderstanding from the outside as some sort of personal savior sitting on a cloud. Zen, in the American grain, reinforced my assumptions that I could pull myself up by my own bootstraps into enlightenment. Sit still, crack your koans, and see into the ultimate reality of things—rightly or wrongly, that was the message I took from Zen, as did many of the other folks in the zendo with me.

Unfortunately, I found out that it didn't work so well for me in practice. All that meditation brought me face to face with my reality, and what I found was a lot less pretty and a lot more irreparably flawed than I'd been led to believe. There wasn't going to be any glorious Zen experience transforming my basic egocentricity into enlightenment. The I that I am can't hope to become selfless on its own: it only exists to reinforce itself, and it will use any means, including telling itself cute little stories about what a good Zennist it is, in order to keep on keeping on.

But don't get me wrong: meditation can definitely be helpful. It was meditation as much as anything that allowed me to wake up initially and see what I was really like. I don't think I'd be a Pure Lander today if I hadn't spent all that time pursuing self-power paths. And many believe that meditation is also a good method for reducing everyday stress and lowering your blood pressure. But there was a limit to how far meditation could take me: I might become outwardly calmer and more aware but inside I was always still the false me. Likewise, while I've met many wise Buddhists of various sects whose practice and integrity I respect, I've never seen anything to convince me that the complete, unsurpassed, perfect enlightenment as described in the traditional texts is a potential achievement in this life. Worse yet, many major teachers believed to be awakened by their communities have gone down in flames as shameful scandals came to light.

So, since the Buddha-mind may be unattainable by my own efforts, and meditation doesn't seem able to carry me all the way to the other shore, Shinran suddenly seems like the most reasonable guy on the block. It's like Shinran said in the *Tannisho:* I don't know if nembutsu will cause me to go to the Pure Land or fall into Hell, but there are no other realistic options available to someone like me. So I'm going to go ahead and chant and express my relief at finding a path that was created for failures such as myself. I guess I'm going to end up a sore-throated Buddhist instead of a hard-assed one.

Our Debt to the Foundresses of Jodo Shinshu

For me as a Shin Buddhist, one of the most important parts of living the spiritual life is learning to look away from myself to see all the factors that go into providing me with life. All of my accomplishments only come about because of the efforts of others. Surely the most important of these people is my wife, whose loving presence is the condition that allows me to have a happy, stable life—and who also provided financial support to our household while I impoverished us through my graduate school education.

In Shin, we usually talk about our gratitude to Shinran, founder of our tradition. However, I think we should also acknowledge that Shin only exists because of the efforts of women, a fact that has largely been overlooked by history. Shinran's insights were substantial, but more than anything it was the example that he set by marrying and raising a family which demonstrated that laypeople could lead an authentic religious life. His partner in this endeavor was his wife Eshinni. She was the woman strong enough in will and faith to endure exile with Shinran, to support him financially while he wrote the treatises that have come down to us today, and to raise the family that went on to become the Honganji lineage, the primary guardians of the Shin legacy. Without her, would Shinran have been able to sustain his life and work during his exile? Would his teachings have lasted long enough to take deep root in Japan, eventually to be transmitted to us in the West? It seems doubtful to me. When I think of Eshinni, she seems to me to be the co-founder of Jodo Shinshu along with Shinran.

Shinran is often cited as the founder of the Honganji school, the main tradition that derives from his teachings. But this is not correct. Shinran did not intend to create a new school of Buddhism, and in fact he died in relative obscurity. The Honganji temple (whose name means Primal Vow Temple) was founded in Kyoto by his daughter, Kakushinni, who cared for him during his final years. It was her devotion and hard work that sowed the seeds for Honganji to become such a major force in Japanese history. Later, Honganji became the vehicle that brought Shin Buddhism to Hawaii, the Americas, Europe, and Australia. I think it can be simply stated that if there had been no Kakushinni, there would be no Honganji, and perhaps therefore no lasting legacy of Shinran in the world. In an important way, Kakushinni is the true founder of Honganji, just as Eshinni is truly the co-founder of Jodo Shinshu.

Our debt to Shinran is deep, but surely our debt to Eshinni and Kakushinni goes just as deep. Remembering to honor them and the countless unnamed women who have nurtured Jodo Shinshu up to the present day should keep us humble about the workings of history.

For every saint that we recognize, so many others have gone unremembered.

Incomplete Nembutsu, Open-Ended Gratitude

THERE IS A CURIOUS PART of the *Shoshinge Wasan* that I have always pondered. The *Shoshinge* is the most important Shin chant, composed by Shinran and included in his magnum opus, *Kyogyoshinsho*. When we chant the *Shoshinge*, it is followed by *wasan* (hymns) also composed by Shinran, interspersed with repetitions of Namo Amidan Bu, an alternative form of Namu Amida Butsu. It is this nembutsu that has been drawing my attention back again and again. There is something unusual about it. Here it is:

Namo Amidan Bu
Namo Amidan Bu
Namo Amidan Bu
Namo Amidan Bu
Namo Amidan Bu
Namo Amidan Bu
Na

It is customary to end Sutra chants with six nembutsu. But the *Shoshinge Wasan* adds an extra syllable at the very end: *Na*. This is what has been working in my mind. Why is there that single *Na* left to hang unfinished after every round? It recurs six times in the Wasan, sticking its neck out and never followed by the rest of the nembutsu, not even a lowly *mo*.

Here is what it means to me. I think that this *Na* is the heart of Shin Buddhism. That may seem strange for such an insignificant syllable—heck, it's not even *Bu,* at least that would be "Buddha." But *Na* is really where it all begins and ends. This *Na* marks an incomplete nembutsu, an open-ended chant that widens in the silence to embrace the world and all things. If *Na* isn't followed by "*-mo Amidan Bu,*" then whatever we say or do afterward becomes itself the completion of this nembutsu. *Na* on its own means that our ordinary speech and actions become nembutsu themselves. It invites us to use our whole lives to express gratitude for all that we receive.

The incomplete nembutsu also points to the fact that we can never hope to fully express the perfection of thankfulness. We are foolish beings, incapable of truly knowing the extent of the debt that we owe for our lives and awakening. The best we can do is sense the deep ocean of compassion that embraces us, and utter nembutsu in return. *Na* without the *mo* means that to the end of our lives, we can never fully repay our debts, that our expression of gratitude is always left incomplete. Being unable to repay them, we are released from the necessity of doing so, freed to simply say the nembutsu that rises in our hearts and do the best we can, day by day.

Finally, *Na* on its own expresses the heart of the Primal Vow. In the eighteenth of his vows, the bodhisattva who would become Amida promised to free all beings who call on him. For Shinran, this call comes at the moment of shinjin, which is time at its ultimate limit, the instant of turning the self over to Other Power. Traditionally, Pure Land Buddhists have believed that it took ten utterances of the nembutsu to fulfill the requirements of the Eighteenth Vow. But as I understand Shinran, shinjin is not measured by tens. It is a moment of infinite brevity. It is the very beginning of the nembutsu, the instant when we are moved to open our mouths and say the nembutsu.

Liberation occurs with *Na*—and all the rest, "-mu Amida Butsu," is our expression of thanksgiving for what has just been received.

Shin without Amida

FOR SEVERAL YEARS Reverend Taitetsu Unno has held summer Shin retreats at the Barre Center for Buddhist Studies in Massachusetts, and my wife and I attend when possible. Something struck me on the second day of one of those retreats. We'd been there for a whole day, including three extended formal gatherings, and not once had we discussed Amida Buddha. Amida hadn't even been mentioned—if you don't count the Buddha's inclusion in the nembutsu.

Meanwhile we'd discussed the purpose of chanting, the need for humility and gratitude, the importance of genuineness, the concept of being embraced just as we are, and interconnection—plus we'd found a full hour and a half to tell funny stories about cats. When I realized that we'd been holding a completely Shin retreat, with lots of deep discussion and relevant stories, it really made me think.

We could've easily gone the entire retreat without talking about Amida Buddha or the Pure Land in any sort of formal or traditional way. No one had been urged to "believe in" Amida, or to expect the Pure Land after death. All our discussions centered on life here and now, waking up to the reality of our imperfection contained within the web of boundless life. It really brought home to me how much more there is to Shin Buddhism. Ultimately, Amida and the Pure Land are pointers to the truth, symbols and teachings that are not the point in themselves.

Of course, as soon as I pointed this out to Dr. Unno, he immediately began the next session with a discussion of Amida Buddha! That's life for you. But he took pains to make it clear that Amida is not a person or an object, Amida is the awakening to reality itself. One poem by a myokonin (I think it was Saichi) really stayed with me:

Eighty-four thousand delusions
Eighty-four thousand Amida Buddhas
Namu Amida Butsu!

Dr. Unno said there are "eighty-four thousand" Amidas (really, a number representing infinity)—one for every possible human delusion. This goes far beyond a conventional understanding of Amida as a particular buddha and deserves careful thought.

Another incident from one of these retreats also stands out. The first night of the retreat, I realized I didn't have enough videotapes for my camcorder. My wife and I took a jaunt down to Worcester to buy some more. On the way back, I was concerned that we wouldn't return in time to meet with Reverend Mark Unno, Tai Unno's son who was assisting with the retreat and had requested a short private audience with all the participants. I got stuck behind a really slow car on the little two-lane roads that lead back to Barre and my anxiety level kept going up as the minutes drained away.

Finally he turned off and I put the pedal down, relieved to be back in control.

Sure enough, a moment later there were blue lights flashing in my rear-view mirror.

Getting a ticket was a real concern to me. I was behind on credit card payments and I wasn't earning much money as a grad student during the summer break. I literally couldn't pay a speeding ticket, plus it might affect my insurance premium. When the officer told me she'd clocked me doing 62 in a 45 mph zone, I was really stunned, I had no idea I'd gone that fast. Things didn't look good.

But then unexpectedly she let me off with a warning, choosing not to write me a $180 ticket. I was so surprised and grateful that "Namu Amida Butsu" popped out. I drove back under the speed limit to the retreat center, and somehow we were there with plenty of time before the interview after all.

Reflecting on this, it seemed to mirror the way in which the Pure Land works. Acting impetuously, overcome by resentment at the slow driver and attachment to the idea of being on time, I committed a crime and the karmic consequences came to bear with startling immediacy. I was confronted with my wrongdoing and the likelihood that I would pay for it. But suddenly I was released from danger and sent on my way. Afterward, I didn't have anything that I hadn't already had—the $180 I didn't lose wasn't anything more than what I'd started with. And yet suddenly it was as if I'd just been given that money (as well as the forgiveness for my misdeed) for free. The non-fine now seemed like a gift, and as I drove back to Barre the night seemed transformed because now I could enjoy it without the cloud of a ticket hanging over my head.

In a way, it is the same with the Pure Land. In the sutra stories, Amida has already secured our liberation. Though we don't perceive it, the light of infinite compassion is constantly embracing us.

But we fail to appreciate it and all that we are given. By all that we are given, I mean every aspect of the universe that makes our lives possible. But then one day someone awakens us to what we already have, to the freedom inherent in *shunyata,* to the Pure Land. We turn around and discover that everything we have taken for granted is actually a wondrous gift that invites our gratitude and appreciation.

When the trusting heart opens we don't gain anything we didn't already have from eons in the past—and yet, we only truly have it after the awakening provided by Other Power.

It's just like the parable in the *Lotus Sutra* of the pearl of great price: a beggar carries with him a jewel of inestimable value, sewn right into his garments—but he doesn't know about it until someone else reveals it to him.

Our lives are always like this; thankfully, it doesn't always take police sirens to wake us up!

Common Destination

WHEN I WAS *in graduate school my wife a*nd I were always driving junky old cars that our family handed down to us out of pity. Inevitably, some of them died on us and ended up being sold for scrap. I vividly remember visiting a graveyard for cars one morning. Their frames were piled rusting on either side of me as I drove my pick-up truck past them, mildly shocked by the sight. In life these dead cars had all been individuals, with particular personalities, specific owners, their own histories and stories to tell. Some were white, some blue, some black, some red. Some had been fancy cars, some were hard-working vehicles, some were lemons from the start. Many had been loved and many had been mistreated. But however they'd appeared during their days of service, they all ended up at the same place, decomposing together without distinctions.

As I looked across that sea of junked cars, I began to wonder what would happen to our society if we ran our own graveyards this way. What if instead of burying our dead or cremating them, we took them to open-air cemeteries where they rotted in plain sight, stacked in row after undifferentiated row: "Look, there's Donald Trump next to that homeless woman from over on Broadway. There's Jesse Helms, and I think that's Jesse Jackson's arm next to him. There's Osama bin Laden, there's George W. Bush, there's the Dalai Lama, there's my next-door neighbor." Everybody, every single person, jumbled together right in plain view. The truth of impermanence (and our non-differentiation) brought home in an undeniable way.

If this were how we did things, it would mean that I would've had to go and watch my grandmother's corpse laid out in that charnel ground, her body disintegrating day by day. At first the thought was unbearable to me. But then I began to wonder whether that might actually have been the better way to do it.

Seeing my grandmother's dead body out in the open, under the blue sky, among the bones of previous generations, might've been just what I needed to come to terms with her absence. The way our society handles death these days is to take it away, put it out of sight, only offering brief prettified glimpses at carefully scripted moments: laid out as if asleep at the funeral home, wearing special make-up for the dead; artificially beatific in the church, held together by chemicals after a normal corpse would've begun to smell ripe; peaceful at last beside the gravesite, ready to rest in the comforting ground. If she'd been treated like a worn-out car, I would've had to come to terms with her really being gone, gone for good, as she naturally transitioned bit by bit from her familiar form into her constituent parts and then into dirt and bones.

Who's to say there might not be some benefit in such a custom, both for the grieving individuals and the contemplating society at large?

After all, whether we want to display it openly or not, we all end up there together at the end of the road, just so much scrap material waiting to be recycled.

All Beings Have Bush-Nature

W E'RE PERHAPS USED TO hearing about how all beings have Buddha-nature, the inherent capacity to become a Buddha, and even the idea that in some way we are already buddhas right now. The Pure Land path assures us that all beings will in fact achieve eventual liberation. But it seems to me that Shin also strives to awaken us to our *Mara*-nature. Mara is the Buddhist embodiment of all the delusions: ignorance, fear, greed, anger, hatred. The strange thing about Shin Buddhism is that it insists that by waking up to our Mara-nature, we become aware of Amida's embracing Other Power, which Shinran equates with Buddha-nature. Mara-nature and Buddha-nature appear simultaneously in the moment of shinjin.

To most of us, Buddha-nature is too abstract to really identify with. But if Mara-nature provides a way to discover Buddha-nature, than perhaps we can start there. For those of us who found George W. Bush to be a rather Mara-ish figure, perhaps it would help to reflect on the idea that we all have Bush-nature. No matter how much we may dislike George Bush, all of the flaws we see in him are also present, to some degree, in ourselves. Had I been born into his situation and experienced his upbringing and karmic circumstances, mightn't I be more or less the same as him? I don't think Bush's actions are *excusable* due to our common foolishness, but they are *understandable,* and we can hope for a measure of humility as we argue against the policies he created. With his karmic and historical background in mind his actions become more comprehensible—and what's more, until we are thrust into a situation of great power, responsibility, and complexity, it is vain to think we really know how we'd react or what ends we'd be driven to. While wishing to do good, I can easily imagine that I might nonetheless end up causing great harm and misery.

Our political opponents aren't our ultimate enemies: the real problem is the same greed and delusion that we find within ourselves. Contemplating my Bush-nature, I see how he and I are the same, both seeking security and vainly grasping at things we think will provide us happiness in this fleeting world.

One of the famous stories in the Pure Land tradition is about Prince Ajatasatru, an evil dictator who illegally seized power and began to carry out a series of inhumane detentions. But Shinran said that in fact Ajatasatru was actually a bodhisattva in disguise. Through his actions, the prince led to the *Contemplation of Amida Sutra* being created, one of the three main Pure Land scriptures. Hard as it is to believe that Bush might be a bodhisattva, how are we to know for sure? Perhaps if he plays that role by allowing us to more easily see the follies of relying on pride and dualistic thinking, he may be the vehicle for someone's awakening.

The qualities that we dislike in someone, such as George Bush, are present in each of us. As I think about this matter further, it seems important to also recognize that in addition to me having Bush-nature, George Bush has Jeff-nature. Or Abe-nature, Kristen-nature, or you-nature. There is no essential difference between us and those we view as opponents. The qualities we admire about ourselves can be found to some degree in just about anyone, and the qualities we dislike about others surely lurk to some extent in our own personalities. Saying that George Bush and I both have Buddha-nature is very abstract—but saying that I have Bush-nature, and that he has Jeff-nature, brings the point home to me very clearly.

I'm not trying to pretend that we're all the same, or that our differences aren't significant. What makes Bush himself and not me is that the Bush-nature that we share is much stronger in him, while my Jeff-nature is much stronger in me. But that can change—I can become more like him, or he can become more like me. Or we could say that Bush-nature can change, so that if he changes, what it means to have Bush-nature will change as well. If we consider others or ourselves to be static individuals, we miss the constant play of emptiness and cut off the potential for development and change that exists in each of us at every moment. That's really what the Buddhist insight into emptiness amounts to: great potentiality, ever present.

Shantideva, the eighth-century Indian Buddhist sage, said in his *Way of the Bodhisattva*:

Those desiring speedily to be
A refuge for themselves and other beings
Should interchange the terms of "I" and "other,"
And thus embrace a sacred mystery.

Embracing the sacred mystery of my Bush-nature, I try to put aside my horror at his actions. Recognizing his Jeff-nature, I try to see him as my kinsman, as we interdependently co-arise in each moment.

Shantideva also says:

Hands and other limbs
Are thought of as the members of a body.
Shall we not consider others likewise—
Limbs and members of a living whole?

Exchanging self and other, I still want to protest the misguided actions of the government. I still want to work against the radical agenda that has been doing so much damage, in America and abroad. And I still want to vote for more compassionate and level-headed politicians. But in doing so, I don't want to lose sight of the way in which Bush and I constitute members in the same living whole. I don't want to see him cut out of the body of humanity; what I want is to see him change, either through a change in personality or a change in his access to power.

In the Pure Land, all beings are reconciled. Amida's light embraces everyone unconditionally and brings them all to the Pure Land, whether or not they are currently Buddhist. Ultimately, everyone gets there. Bush has no way of removing himself, or being removed by me or anyone else, from the living whole. In the end, George Bush, Saddam Hussein, Osama bin Laden, all the devils and saints of history, all the mediocre forgotten ones, and me, all end up in the Pure Land, liberated from our foolish ignorance and painful egocentricity. As long as we can keep that in mind, we can hope to agitate for change while not losing sight of the inner togetherness that we share with our political opponents.

Amida Is Foolish Too

THE FAMOUS Shin myokonin Saichi wrote:

> The world is foolish, I am foolish,
> Amida is foolish too;
> No matter, the parent-like Buddha relieves foolishness,
> "Namu-Amida-Butsu."

Amida is foolish too. This is a statement perhaps without parallel in religion. It is a relatively easy thing to say that the world is foolish. Many people have also woken up to their own foolishness. But to realize that the source of one's salvation, be it God or Buddha or whatever, is *also* foolish—*that* is a revolutionary thing.

What does Saichi mean here? I can't claim to know for sure. But when I reflect it seems to me that Amida is foolish because Amida is never apart from us, who are foolish, and all the world, which is foolish too. Amida participates in our foolishness in order to relieve it. Amida doesn't cast sinners out in anger. Those who are hardest to reach are given the lion's share of Amida's compassionate attention.

I can't pretend to be this compassionate. I prefer to give my love and affection to those who return it. I'm no Buddha. But living in Amida's light, I do wish for others to experience happiness and peace, even those who dislike me or would do me harm. Perhaps we aren't friends now, but there's always the future. So much has changed in my life, including the 180-degree shift in my thinking about Pure Land Buddhism's worth.

It makes me hold back on saying "never."

Somehow the foolish Amida will help this foolish self to embrace everyone equally.

Deep Hearing

I N SHIN, we frequently talk about deep hearing. It is often considered the main religious activity of Shin followers. Based on remarks that some people have made to me, I think that misunderstandings of deep hearing must pop up from time to time. Bearing in mind that I too struggle to understand the many profound concepts found within Buddhism, I would like to offer my own understanding of deep hearing so that it might help others who are confused.

The primary mistake that I see some people committing is the classification of deep hearing as *a practice one performs.* I can sympathize with those who wish to find some sort of plan of action in the concept of deep hearing. Shin Buddhism's message—that we are fine just as we all are, without any need for achievement—is as radical today as it was during Shinran's time. Everything within us cries out for a method, a practice, a tool—something to latch on to and use in order to transform ourselves into someone or something we wish we were. The idea of letting go of methods and allowing Dharma to simply work on us is frightening. If we are people of self-confidence, that self-confidence encourages us to keep pulling ourselves up by our own bootstraps. If we are people of self-doubt, that self-doubt whispers to us that we aren't going to be able to find buddhahood. It's easy to understand why the Chinese Pure Land teacher Tan-luan said that the Pure Land way is easy, but few enter it.

Those who see deep hearing as a practice are only understanding it partially. I think the mistake must arise from the fact that deep hearing is a process. But it is not a process of our ignorant selves working to become enlightened. Rather, it is a process performed by the natural unfolding of the Dharma in each of our lives. It isn't that we should strive to hear the Dharma, to perceive the call of Amida telling us that everything is alright just as it is. Rather, hearing comes about when we put down our efforts and let the Dharma work on us without interference.

Deep hearing often has three stages. The first is when we listen to others telling us about the Dharma. Although we only understand things partially, out of faith we go back again and again to encounter the Dharma, until it sinks into our bones. We listen to the stories and teachings of the tradition, soaking in the Dharma over the course of a lifetime until we are thoroughly wet. The call that liberates is already working on us, driving us to seek out the Dharma and reflect on it.

Eventually, deep hearing moves into a second stage. We are led to drop our striving and rely on Amida alone. At this moment, we deeply hear the call of Other Power telling us that just as we are, we are welcomed into the Land of Bliss, never to be abandoned. Here nembutsu truly becomes a shout of joyful gratitude, rather than a cry for help.

In the third stage of deep hearing, the first two are assimilated.

We continue to seek out the Dharma and receive solace from it, deeply listening to the wisdom of our teachers and peers. And we hear the promise of Amida when we are led to say nembutsu, ever renewing our remembrance of the gift of Other Power. Finally, we also perceive the call and presence of Amida in all things. Just as the birds, trees, rivers, and all things in the Pure Land preach the Dharma, so through deep hearing we encounter the ways in which all phenomena constantly demonstrate the Dharma to us.

All of this, each stage, is brought about by the process of Other Power's working on us through deep hearing.

May we always keep our ears open to the Dharma, right now and in every situation.

Flowers of the Pure Land

MANY SHIN COMMENTATORS have drawn attention to a passage in the *Smaller Pure Land Sutra* about flowers in the Land of Bliss emitting brilliant lights:

> In the ponds are lotuses as large as chariot-wheels—the blue ones radiating a blue light, the yellow a yellow light, the red a red light, and the white a white light. They are all marvelous and beautiful, fragrant and pure.

According to the commentators, this passage indicates that all people, just as they are, are worthy and equal. Blue flowers put out blue light, yellow flowers put out yellow light, and all are considered marvelous and beautiful. Just so, people may be white or black, short or tall, Japanese or American, successful or struggling, but all are equally good just as they are. Learning to appreciate the diversity of people as they are, as Amida does, is part of opening up to the Pure Land in this life.

This teaching has always been very important to me. However, there is an aspect of the *Contemplation of Amida Sutra,* another of the three main Pure Land scriptures, that has frequently confounded me. This sutra describes the flowers of the Pure Land in the exact opposite way:

> From the beryl-colored blossoms and leaves issues forth a golden light. From the crystal-colored issues forth a crimson light. From the agate-colored issues forth a sapphire light. From the sapphire-colored issues a green pearl light.

Here the flowers specifically don't emit their own color, they emit lights of other colors. So which is it: do flowers in the Land of Bliss shine with their own beautiful colors just as they are, or do they glow with the light of other hues? I have thought a lot about this matter. Obviously, this isn't meant to be taken literally. But what are the lessons being provided here?

For me, I decided that the *Smaller Sutra* offers a teaching on the equality of all beings, and their value just as they are, without having to undergo strenuous exercises in the attempt to change into buddhas. And that the *Contemplation Sutra* offers a teaching on interconnectedness, the inner togetherness that all beings share as our fundamental nature. All things in the universe arise together and rely on one another, thus flowers shine with the color of other blossoms and people display traits of each other.

Significantly, the flowers in the *Smaller Sutra* are described in biological terms: their species and local environment are mentioned. Whereas in the *Contemplation Sutra,* the flowers are described in terms of precious gemstones. This points to the source of this teaching: the jeweled net of Indra, the Buddhist symbol of the interconnection and interpenetration of all things in the universe. Each jewel in the net reflects all the other jewels, and in those reflections are the reflections of all the jewels being reflected, and so on, producing a holographic vision of the infinite dependent co-origination and simultaneous arising of all things. Thus in each person abides the entire universe, and each of us is connected to every bit of stuff that exists. This, of course, is inner togetherness.

In the end, these are not contradictory descriptions. The Pure Land exists to lead us to the truth of things as they are—it is not a static place frozen in time, but a skillful means that reveals itself to us in multiple forms so that we can discover the way of liberation. When the flowers shine with their own simple lights, they show us that we have value whoever we are, and that others too must be appreciated for their inherent value—we are each good in our individuality. And when the flowers shine with the light of other colors, they show us that we are not simply isolated individuals, but nexuses of all things in the universe, connected and dependent on one another—we are all good in our togetherness.

Both lights shine on us effortlessly from the flowers of the Pure Land… and from the flowers of this world, if we can learn to look deeply into them and see the teachings they offer us.

A Parcel of Vain Strivings

HENRY DAVID THOREAU, one of the first Americans to express an interest in Buddhism, once wrote: "I am a parcel of vain strivings tied / by a chance bond together."

I've always thought this sentiment perfectly expressed the Buddhist understanding of the self. There is no essence to a person, no soul or indestructible kernel lurking somewhere hidden in the body or mind. Rather, we are intersections where things that are *not* essentially us—blood, bone, neurons, flesh, and food, water, parental care, and other supporting elements—meet for a moment. Mentally, we are a flux, probably with more vain strivings than noble impulses. Chance and karma bring all of these together for a little while, then untie the knot again and what was "me" goes spiraling off in all directions, perhaps to come together in new configurations somewhere else.

For some, the self is something to be clung to with all one's might, the crutch upon which one leans when all else is taken away.

And for others, God is another object of clinging, a kind of self writ large.

But for me, the fact that we are nothing more than a temporary nexus of non-self elements, assembled by causes and conditions, chance and karma, is a source of wonder and awe. The philosopher Ludwig Wittgenstein seems to have experienced something similar:

> I believe the best way of describing [my deepest experience] is to say that when I have it I wonder at the existence of the world. And I am then inclined to use such phrases as "how extraordinary that anything should exist" or "how extraordinary that the world should exist."

How extraordinary indeed! Faced with something so incredible as this—the unlikely existence of myself and the world—words fail me. What else can I do but utter nembutsu? It isn't that I fully perceive the mystery of all things and simply say nembutsu in satisfied gratitude. It's quite the opposite—I receive the merest glimpse into how staggeringly unlikely, and therefore how deeply precious, our lives are. The nembutsu is my response because, as Shinran says at the end of the first part of the *Tannisho*, "The meaning of the nembutsu is that it is beyond all logic. For it is beyond calculation, beyond explanation, and beyond understanding."

The wonder I feel at there being *something*, rather than nothing, is so large it goes beyond my calculation, beyond the possibility of my making an explanation, far beyond my understanding. That a parcel of vain strivings should appear in this world and be able to experience love, life, loss, beauty, growth—it is beyond my ability to ever fully comprehend. And that it should be embraced by infinite wisdom and compassion beyond the self and delivered to awakening and bliss—it is truly wondrous.

My only hope of expressing these feelings is through the nembutsu, the voice of buddha-nature itself.

Whatever Land,
Whatever Body

'M NOT A PRIEST. I'm not even a particularly good Buddhist. And I'm certainly not of Japanese descent. Often, I wonder what right I have to speak for Shin Buddhism. Who am I to put my words out in front of the world as if I'm an authority? It really worries me that sticking my neck out like this somehow implies a sort of specialness on my part that I utterly lack.

And yet, if we who have been touched by the beauty and liberating power of the Shin tradition don't offer our stories, then what will become of the Buddha's message of hope?

There is a passage from Shinran's writings that gives me courage even as I interrogate myself and my hubris at daring to claim a small part in that tradition.

> From this day to the very end of time, wherever you are, give praise to the Vow, and wherever you may go, encourage others to hear it. Whatever body and land you may be born into as your recompense, whatever the conditions for

teaching others, your work is the same as Amida Buddha's, without any difference. This aspiration is boundless; may the Buddha recognize and know this.

This quote is tucked away in a minor yet meaningful work, called *Gutoku's Notes.* It could perhaps be translated more viscerally as "Scribblings of a Bald-headed Fool." Personally, I think Shinran would approve of that title.

When I read this passage, it never fails to move me. It is as if Shinran is speaking right to me and to the others who struggle to articulate the wonder of Amida's never-abandoning power in a world that is both utterly unlike anything Shinran ever imagined, and yet still so stuck in exactly the same delusions and foibles that he encountered in others and in himself. From Shinran's time eight hundred years ago until today and the end of time, wherever we may be, he encourages us to praise the liberating Vow of Amida and share it with others.

In my own case, I have been born into a rather short and stout body, in a land far from Japan that has many problems and successes. It may be the result of good karma, or, quite more likely, some karma that is less than respectable. My conditions for teaching aren't perfect, but then again I have experienced a great many blessings that others in this age will never have the benefit of. No matter. If Shinran is to be believed, even my efforts and yours are the same as Amida's. That's quite a statement. Not *similar* to Amida's—but *the same,* without any difference. This is a deeply empowering message.

Amida's light is boundless. There is nowhere it does not shine and no one it does not illuminate, no matter what they look like, what language they speak, or what land they inhabit. Each of us can go forth to share with others the joy that we receive from Shin Buddhism and the reality of our inner togetherness.

So: Don't let yourself be held back—go ahead and share.

Every time you do, Shinran is smiling, pleased that the teaching goes on to open hearts anew.

All Wars Are World Wars

E VERY COUNTRY is no more than a few degrees of separation from any conflict. In this way, all wars are world wars. In the contemporary situation, it is easy to see how the entire world is always involved in every war. But as Buddhists, we should recognize that this has always been the case: every war, in every period, is always a world war. There is no such thing as an isolated conflict. All things arise together and are completely interconnected, interpenetrating to a degree impossible for the foolish human mind to fully comprehend. What affects the strangers in Iraq, for instance, affects me and every other person on the planet, even if I don't immediately perceive the effects. Shatter one gemstone in Indra's net, and the trauma is reflected in all.

If we turn away from conflict, thinking we can escape the pain that others experience, we are mistaken about how the universe operates, and we betray the bodhisattva vow. There is nowhere that one can go in samsara to get away from our connection to the sufferings of others.

The only thing I can do is turn toward the pain that others feel and say, "This involves me too. When you hurt, so do I."

The Tip of the Iceberg

T HE NEMBUTSU is the way in which we express our appreciation, shallow or deep, for all the myriad unknowable gifts of
this life. Accordingly, I have been thinking recently about
another myokonin story.

There was a myokonin who said the nembutsu constantly out of
joy and gratitude. The only dark spot in his life was that when he
went to light the stove, he couldn't say nembutsu, because he had
to blow on the spark to make the fire catch. Then one day he discovered that he could use bellows to fan the flame, meaning that he
didn't have to stop saying nembutsu for even as short a time as it
took to light the fire. This discovery gave him great happiness.

Like all myokonin stories, there is great charm to this tale of simple gratitude and joyfulness. I don't want to criticize such a person
of deep faith—but I do want to say that my understanding is a little
different. To me, when the nembutsu sinks into your bones, every
action can become a form of thanksgiving. Thus blowing on the fire
could be expressing one's gratitude, even if it isn't a verbalized

nembutsu in a strict sense. The nembutsu that we say, that others can hear, is only the tip of the shinjin iceberg; the nembutsu we recite is only the most visible sign of the working of Other Power within the shadowy ego-self. That inner working of shinjin may show through as nembutsu, but it can also show through in a hug, a gift, a kind word, laughter.

Nembutsu is a vital avenue for expressing our faith, but it need not be taken for the whole iceberg. There's really no limit to the possibilities of expression of the trusting heart.

From Sincerity to Compassion

SEE THE PROCESS of Other Power penetrating and opening our lives as having four steps, which I relate to the teaching in the Eighteenth Vow—described in the story of the *Larger Pure Land Sutra*—that the true mind has three elements: sincerity, trust, and aspiration for birth in the Pure Land along with all beings. Sincerity is the beginning of the Shin path. When we reflect on ourselves honestly, we discover that we are not as good as we habitually think we are. In fact, we find that our efforts rarely succeed to the degree we would like, and that in the course of each day we create many problems for ourselves and others, intentionally or otherwise. No matter how hard we try, ego always arises and makes a mess of things. Sincerity is the willingness to see things as they are, which sometimes takes a certain amount of courage. One has to let go of pride in order to pry the lid off our self-images and look into the darkness hiding inside. I think that sincerity has some linkage to the concept of mindfulness often employed by other schools of Buddhism.

Through sincerely examining the self, we move to the next step in the process: humility. Awakened by Amida's light of wisdom to our self-centeredness, we realize the foolishness of our internal narratives of self-aggrandizement. We find that the self is a rather silly thing, puffed up far beyond its actual capacities, but nevertheless able to cause considerable harm. As we see just how deluded we really are, we are simultaneously awakened to Amida's compassionate embrace. No matter how foolish or evil we may be, Other Power constantly provides us with what we need to live and discover true reality in each moment. Letting go of the inadequate ego-self, we relax as Amida's power flows through us, bringing us from sincerity to humility to deep entrusting. Humility and trust go hand in hand, forming the second part of the true trusting mind. Shinjin is another name for this development of humility-entrusting.

Once one has been awakened to the vast incalculable support of Other Power underpinning our lives, we can see that all things are truly interconnected. Knowing the bonds of interdependent co-arising that knit us into the fabric of the universe along with all other beings, we begin to develop the quality of compassion. In traditional terms, this can be expressed as the aspiration to achieve the Pure Land, because the reason a bodhisattva wishes to go to the Pure Land is in order to become a buddha and return to the world to alleviate suffering. Furthermore, in Pure Land Buddhism specifically, we talk about the symbiosis of all life and the desire to be awakened in the Pure Land together with all other living things. Thus in coming to the final part of the process, having sincerely admitted our limitations, renounced self-power, and gained the joy of entrusting, we express our gratitude through acts of compassionate service to others. The happiness that I feel when I reflect on Amida's gift cannot be contained—it spills out spontaneously and is channeled both through chanting nembutsu and through using my resources to be good to others.

Although I can't claim to be good or joyful all the time, I think

Other Power does lead me to do more good than I would if I were as ego-bound as before I encountered the Vow. Perhaps more significant, relying on Other Power allows me to avoid a certain amount of unskillful behavior that I would have otherwise rushed into. Even though I fall back on myself time and again and create difficulties, Amida has got a hold of me and always draws me back.

I'm thankful for being given the opportunity to love and be loved by others, and to express that love through service. The little good I do in this world is, truly, the least I can do in return, but it is what I can do.

Receiving the Gift

Life in North America is not perfect, but for me at least it is relatively comfortable and empowered. Though it may be a cliché, innumerable people fought and died so that I would be able to exercise the freedoms I enjoy. Through no work of my own, unearned, I receive this precious gift. My family history includes slave-owners and Klan members, men who opposed allowing others to exercise these same rights. I haven't done anything to earn the right to vote, or to be worthy of my access to healthcare, security, housing, and other aspects of North American life that I benefit from.

I don't accept that my access to these things is simply the working of good karma: on no level can I discover a way in which I am better than those who lack these privileges, nor do I have confidence that I was better once upon a time in a life I can't recall. When I look inside, I don't find anything upon which to assert such a claim. As I examine the world, it seems that circumstances usually dictate our behaviors, even if to a certain degree some of our circumstances are the result of our previous actions. I cannot lay claim to any good karma that provides me with my relatively cushy life, because my actions are the result of others working for my benefit, of choices I've made with imperfect knowledge of the situation, of motivations I can hardly pretend are free of egoism, whether I perceive it or not.

Shinran said that he could not know what good or evil were: if he were fully awakened like Amida then he could perceive all the contingencies of each situation and thus make a truly moral or immoral choice, but being a foolish being he had no hope of practicing true goodness. I agree. While I work to do good as best I know it, I can't claim any real credit for it, nor can I pretend that I know for certain that the results of my actions will truly be good. All I can do is try my best, rely on Amida, and let things work the way they will.

Receiving benefits that I can't in good conscience claim as my own, I am motivated to try to make sure that others receive such gifts as well. And I remember that while political, social, and economic benefits are crucial, even the drawing of breath from moment to moment is a gift provided by the universe through no action of my own.

All actions are manifestations of Other Power: breathing is Other Power, nembutsu is Other Power, voting is Other Power.

Two Aspects of Amida

ONE OF SHINRAN'S DOCTRINES is the idea of two Amidas. Essentially, Shinran says that the Dharmakaya, the ultimate interconnected reality of all things, is so incredible that human minds have difficulty understanding it. We might call this aspect of the Dharmakaya "Amida of ultimate reality." It has no form or name and though we can perceive it after a fashion, it is beyond any possible full conception by human beings. But then there is a second Dharmakaya, the form which reality takes on in order to graciously awaken us to the interconnectedness within which we live and love and have our being. This is Dharmakaya for us: it is Amida as a form (Buddha), a view (shinjin), a name (Namu Amida Butsu). These two Dharmakayas, the two Amidas, are the same, but they appear different to us because one is accommodated to our level of understanding.

In Buddhism generally, there is the doctrine of the two truths. The first type of truth is ultimate reality, *shunyata,* emptiness. The second type is conventional truth, the everyday appearance of things we perceive. This second truth is sometimes considered somehow lower or inferior to ultimate truth in some way; some theories even go so far as to say that relative or conventional truth isn't true at all, and that only ultimate truth is real.

We can see the relation between Shinran's two Amidas and the Buddhist doctrine of the two truths. However, they are not identical. For one thing, Amida-for-us isn't a lie or an illusion—Amida's conventional forms directly point to the ultimate truth, and therefore they partake of that reality. "Namu Amida Butsu" is just a phrase... yet it is also so much more than a phrase. "Namu Amida Butsu" is the voice of the universe itself, calling each of us to pause and awaken to the enfolding reality which supports us with wisdom and compassion. The painting of Amida is just colors on a piece of paper, yet it is much more as well: properly understood, this opaque picture becomes a transparent window into our true selves.

Here we see a difference from the venerable saying about the finger and the moon. Buddhist teachers—Shinran included—often admonish us not to mistake the finger that is pointing at the moon for the moon itself. Granted, I doubt anyone ever mistook a finger for a moon, but the lesson here is not to mistake the means that points to truth for the truth itself. In a certain sense, we can say that Amida in form is the finger than points to the greater reality of Amida as limitless interconnection. However, as Shin Buddhists, we affirm the value of not just the moon but also the finger. When the finger points at the moon, it is part of that seamless reality which includes the finger, the moon, the viewer, and all things. The moon may be grander than the finger, but the finger can't be left out of ultimate reality. So too with pictures of Amida and uttered nembutsus: they are a means for encountering the deepest level of truth, but they also participate in that truth.

I know some Buddhists who eschew images of Buddhas,

demanding that we turn away from partial things to encounter the ultimate. There's a certain nobility to this idealist viewpoint, but I think it is misguided. The idea that there is an ultimate reality somehow *apart from* form is incorrect. Form is exactly emptiness; emptiness exactly form. When we look at a Buddha painting or statue, we are looking at emptiness in form. The same could be said about any object: one could theoretically enshrine a pencil or a hubcap or a rock on their altar and make the legitimate claim that it represented emptiness. When asked who was Buddha, the great Chinese Chan teacher Yunmen replied: "A dry feces-covered stick." And he was of course perfectly correct about this.

Yunmen was referring to the ancient Chinese monastic equivalent of used toilet paper, and, while his sentiment was certainly true from a certain angle, I daresay that a wad of used toilet paper would not make a terribly inspiring altar ornament. A Buddha image represents reality as it is, and the Buddha image participates in that reality it points to, modeling for us deluded beings how that reality would look if we were to wake up and embody it in our own lives.

Thus Shinran's concept of the two Amidas provides us with a way to honor both the relative and ultimate levels of reality—and a way to justify using lovely golden Buddha statues, rather than less, shall we say, *awe-inspiring* objects, as Yunmen might have us do…

Reconstituting the Sangha

A WORD WHICH ONE HEARS commonly in Buddhist circles in the West is *Sangha,* which is usually used to label any Buddhist congregation. Yet in some ways, this is actually a novel usage—in Asia, the equivalent word usually refers to the community of ordained monastics and does not include the laypeople. But in Jodo Shinshu Buddhism at least, we have ample reason to truly claim the mantle of Sangha, and in fact have been using the term in this expanded way for a long time.

When we examine the context of the term in the sutras, we find that it has two usages. One is in connection to *bhikkhus* (monks) and *bhikkhunis* (nuns): the bhikkhu-sangha and the bhikkhuni-sangha. This is the main sense that has survived down to today. However, one also finds the term used more generically as *ariya*-sangha: the assembly of noble people who follow the Buddha-way. In this sense, ariya is understood as including all persons who have achieved at least the stage of "stream-enterer," meaning they have advanced to a minimum level of attainment sufficient that they are guaranteed awakening within at most a few lifetimes.

If we wanted to be polite, we could apply the ariya notion of

Sangha to everyone who attends Buddhist functions—after all, who are we to guess at the attainment of other people? However, in the case of Shin followers, it can be more specifically applied. In his writings and letters, Shinran continually emphasized that we who trust in the nembutsu are grasped, never to be abandoned. Our buddhahood is guaranteed; we enter the Pure Land after death and lose all of our karmic hindrances and mental defilements. Better yet, when we receive shinjin in this lifetime, we are already inhabitants of the Pure Land. In fact, Shinran said that "there is no need to wait in anticipation of the moment of death."

Shinran often used the phrase that we are "equal to Maitreya," who is the bodhisattva waiting to be born in this world and become the world's newest Buddha. In other words, those who say the nembutsu are all stream-winners. Prompted by Amida, we have all stepped into the current that leads to awakening, and the flow of Dharma is inexorably bearing us along toward buddhahood.

Before Shinran, people imagined liberation was really only possible for members of the elite monastic communities, which often excluded the handicapped, criminals, women, and other disenfranchised groups. But Shinran made a decisive break, shifting from bhikkhu-sangha consciousness to ariya-sangha consciousness. He understood that it isn't ordination that makes one a part of the Sangha, it is stream-entrance, something achieved by all nembutsu followers. He demonstrated this most concretely when he married Eshinni, turning from the celibate bhikkhu-sangha altogether to affirm the noble sangha as his refuge. And for this, we can all feel grateful.

We too share in this noble Sangha—open once and for all to everyone.

Gratitude for Food

BEFORE WE EAT our meals together, my wife and I put our hands together, bow our heads, and say three nembutsus. It's a quick ritual, easy to do, but powerful. There are few places in our lives where our total reliance on others are more directly revealed than in our encounter with life-sustaining food.

A symbolic number from East Asian Buddhist culture is 88. In eastern Asia it is said that 88 causes and conditions go into the process of bringing a single grain of rice to your plate. And in fact, the character for "rice," almost synonomous in Japan with food, is written with the characters for "ten" and two "eights" to form a representation of eighty-eight (eighty-eight in Japanese is literally "eight-ten-eight"). Such causes include the farmer who planted the seed, the rain that nourished it, the sun that warmed it, the farmhand who harvested it, the driver who brought it to market, the merchant who sold it, and on and on and on. Looking at a grain of rice sitting in our bowl, we see the culmination of 88 different forces working to feed us. Since 88 is a symbol, it really means that innumerable causes and conditions have come together in order to feed and nourish us.

The modern Vietnamese Zen teacher Thich Nhat Hanh instructs his followers to create little rituals of mindfulness. For instance, when the phone rings, breathe three times and return yourself to mindfulness of your surroundings before answering. In a way, our pre-meal nembutsus serve a similar purpose. Saying the nembutsu out of gratitude for our food and all that sustains us naturally leads me to remembrance of Other Power constantly embracing us.

If we don't dine together at any point during the day (an unfortunately frequent occurrence in the lives of two working people), then we sometimes say our nembutsus in bed before going to sleep. We do have a home altar set up with a calligraphy nembutsu and portraits of Shinran and Rennyo, so perhaps this would be the appropriate place for such devotions. But to me, every place and every time is the proper place and time to express our thanks to Amida. There isn't any place or time that Amida isn't continually supporting us, allowing us to live naturally, freeing us from angst about our imperfect selves or future condition.

The truth is, even though I feel great gratitude for the gift of Other Power, my daily grind constantly pulls me away from mindfulness of the Buddha. Therefore, these little acts of programmed nembutsu open a space within which we can hear the call once again. I don't consider them practices, because they aren't "efficacious" in the way that the term *practice* is usually employed by the self-powered schools of Buddhists.

They're just Amida's way of lightly tapping us on the shoulder during the course of our non-stop, hectic lives, reminding us to open our hearts with trust.

Buddhism Is Bullsh*t

HA, GOT YOUR ATTENTION with that title, I bet!

Actually, I'm paraphrasing Reverend Ryo Imamura, a Shin minister and psychotherapist who lives on the West Coast. Here's what Reverend Imamura has to say: "I see Buddhism as being like fertilizer, in that it enriches and nourishes all beliefs and practices without trying to replace them."

That quote comes from "Buddhist and Western Psychotherapies: An Asian American Perspective," published in *The Faces of Buddhism in America.* As you can see, the bullsh*t we're talking about is the fertilizing and nurturing kind, not the falsehood kind. I always loved that the natural fertilizer my mom puts on her garden in Connecticut is euphemistically called "moo dirt." Here's another, similar quote from Reverend Imamura: "I see Buddhism as being like tofu, in that it coexists unobtrusively in any setting and any population without needing to dominate."

I guess if I'd titled this chapter "Buddhism is Tofu," fewer people might have turned right to this chapter...

There's a similarity here to the old Buddhist idea of awakening as the lotus that grows out of the mud of ordinary, deluded life. Lotuses can't bloom unless there is mud, and without bullsh*t or some similar smelly fertilizer, we don't get the crops we live on. Every aspect of life, the pure and the foul, contributes in some way to our existence. Perhaps it wouldn't be entirely inappropriate to sometimes say "Namu bullsh*t" in the same way we say "Namu Amida Butsu."

Preferences, Prejudices, and Mistakes in the Narrative of "Americanized" Shin

THERE'S AN ENDURING, but misguided, assertion in the interpretation of Shin Buddhism in America. Mainly formulated by religious outsiders, it suggests that Jodo Shinshu has become "Christianized," or that Pure Land Buddhism is in some way a species or analog of Christianity in Buddhist guise. How many times have I read or heard someone's first (and often only) reactions to Shin after attending a service: comments about how Christian it seemed, with pews, hymns, organs, and a minister.

The problem with this conceptualization of American Shin can be highlighted by pointing out the comparison with American Judaism. During the same time period that Shin Buddhists were immigrating and adapting to America, Jews were undergoing similar changes. Judaism's history in America begins in 1654, well before Buddhists arrived, but it was in the latter part of the nineteenth century and the earlier decades of the twentieth that Jewish immigration was at its most significant and Americanizing trends became most prominent (and contested!). This is exactly the period when immigrants brought Japanese Buddhism—mainly Jodo Shinshu—to North America.

Jewish practices at the start of this period were very different than they are today. Women were excluded from the main part of the synagogue sanctuary: they sat in the balcony. Services lacked musical instruments and there were no choirs. The congregation was noticeably separated from the *bema,* the raised area where the Torah is stored. But Jewish traditions changed remarkably in response to their new American environment. Today, in many congregations women and men sit together. Organs and other instruments are common, as are choirs. And there has been a movement to bring the congregation and the rabbi and Torah closer together physically, to encourage greater intimacy within the worship space.

American Judaism isn't usually talked about as having been "Christianized" or as being somehow divorced from its roots, despite these and other major innovations. Yet the same sorts of structural changes in North American Shin provoke a nearly uncontested stream of comments that are either critical or bemused. I think the reason must be a sort of unconscious Orientalism on the part of American observers. People look at Judaism as a Western, monotheistic faith, and don't expect it to look significantly different from American Christianity. But Buddhism is expected to look, sound, and feel totally *other.* Indeed, on some level it seems that both anti-Buddhists and people with generally favorable opinions of Buddhism need Buddhism as some sort of ultimate other. For anti-Buddhists, Buddhism plays the role of the demonic other; for people disenchanted with Christianity, it plays the role of the alluring, exotic other. Both impulses tend to fossilize Buddhism into something of the idealized past, and holders of such views feel disturbed when living Buddhism's continuing adaptability to contemporary situations produces a look which fails to meet their Orientalist preferences.

Furthermore, not only are many of the changes in American Shin parallel to accepted changes in American Judaism (and American Islam to some extent too), but some aren't even *American* changes. For instance, the often-remarked-upon "American" adaptation of Shin Sunday Schools is, in fact, an import from Japan, where Sunday Schools were created in the nineteenth century. Likewise, the Young Men's Buddhist Association, a clear analog to the YMCA, was created in Asia and imported to America.

If people only rely on first impressions, it's easy to get the wrong impression. But those who stay and learn more about Shin, particularly those willing to put their preconceived ideas about Buddhism and religion aside, readily find that it is a unique and vital version of the Buddhadharma.

Refugees

WHEN WE SAY that we take refuge in the Buddha, the Dharma, and the Sangha, we acknowledge our status as refugees. A refugee is a person who cannot rest at ease, who is fleeing trouble, strife, violence, fear—which is to say, *dukkha,* suffering. We are refugees from a world steeped in anger, greed, and delusion, seeking asylum in the country of the Buddha, the Pure Land. We turn toward the Pure Land because of the presence of injustice, war, poverty, disease, exploitation, discrimination, and the other marks of samsara, the world of delusion. And we especially seek refuge from our own addiction to the three poisons. Each nembutsu is, in a way, a petition for admittance to a better place, where we can be free from sufferings created by self and others and work instead to increase the happiness of all beings.

Refuge is always extended to those who need it. Amida takes in all the refugees of racism, all the refugees of sexism, all the refugees of homophobia, all the refugees of poverty, all the refugees of illness, all the refugees of violence, all the refugees of sadness, heartache, ennui, confusion, disillusionment, depression, and suffering. And Amida takes in all the refugees of our own racism, all our own sexism, our own wrong treatment of others for whatever reason. Killers and victims, soldiers and civilians, blacks and whites, women and men, gays and homophobes, poor and rich, afflicted and healthy, we all qualify for the refuge of the Pure Land.

Political refugees sadly often find they are unwelcome in their new land and unable to return to the old. But refugees who come to the Pure Land all become full citizens of the Land of Bliss. Nembutsu becomes our national anthem and the Dharma our Constitution. We pledge allegiance as bodhisattvas to do what we can to offer aid to others, to laugh at the foolishness of our self-cherishing, and to retain a mind of grateful awareness for the gift of refuge in our true home. We return to the Old Country of samsara to help bring strangers and loved ones back to refuge with us, or to work for peace and happiness among those who do not realize yet that they too are refugees.

Floating Downriver

KOBAYASHI ISSA, one of Japan's three greatest haiku masters, lived an uneasy life, marked by family trouble and the death of his young children. He is perhaps best known for the poignant poem written after the death of his daughter:

This world of dew
is a world of dew
and yet, and yet...

In only a few words, Issa pours out his conflicted feelings, caught between a fleeting world he knows is both impermanent and painful, and the deep love which prevents him from turning away from it. For millennia Buddhists have struggled with this fundamental human dilemma, different sects and individuals finding their own ways to resolve the tension between the Second Noble Truth—that attachment is the root of suffering—and the persistent demands of the heart. Complacency when times are (temporarily) good is a common phenomenon that Issa gently mocks:

Within this world
we trod upon the roof of hell
enjoying flowers.

And yet, Issa refuses to turn away from the flowers. In this moment, fraught as it is, he finds liberation precisely through the recognition of its beauty and brevity:

Insects on a branch
floating downriver
still singing.

Issa was a Shin Buddhist. Thus when he writes of tiny beings singing as they float precariously in the stream, we should think of Buddhists chanting their gratitude to Amida, the Buddha of infinite compassion and wisdom. His prescription for us weak, imperiled beings is to sing and chant with joy even as the flow of life moves inexorably toward its end.

There is more than a hint here of the Chinese parable about the tiger and cliff. A man traveling across a field encountered a tiger. He fled, the tiger close behind him. Coming to a precipice, he caught hold of the root of a wild vine and swung himself down over the edge. The tiger sniffed at him from above. Trembling, the man looked down to where, far below, another tiger was waiting to eat him. Only the vine sustained him. Two mice, one white and one black, little by little began to gnaw away the vine. The man saw a luscious strawberry near him. Grasping the vine with one hand, he plucked the strawberry with the other.

How sweet it tasted!

The Essence of Shin Buddhism

IT'S SAID that the first two lines of Shinran's *Shoshinge* summarize the essence of Jodo Shinshu Buddhism. That's a pretty heavy weight for just two lines of verse to uphold, especially lines that aren't at first philosophical or revelatory, but when you think about it, it seems to make sense. Here are those famous lines:

I take refuge in the Tathagata of Immeasurable Life!
I entrust myself to the Buddha of Inconceivable Light!

Everything you need for Shin Buddhism is right here. Shinran describes the Buddha of light and life without any possible boundaries or limitations, and utterly beyond the ability of our deluded present minds to fully comprehend. Furthermore, this light and life stands for wisdom and compassion, the two hallmarks of awakening which guide us to liberation from foolishness and egocentricity. In the aspect of Tathagata, Amida embodies reality-as-it-is, while as Buddha, Amida is the being who emerges from ignorance into illumination in that reality.

Perhaps most important of all are the verbs, "taking refuge" and "entrusting." They describe the practice and the mindset of the Shin Buddhist—what we are to do. The wisdom and compassion of Other Power offer us refuge from the storms of samsara, providing the peace and security the Pure Land has always represented in vividly symbolic fashion. By taking that offered refuge, we commit ourselves to finding a better way than that provided by the usual world of greed, competition, hostility, bias, dualism, and delusion. And even though we fall short of the goal, entrusting is the most profound act of the Shin Buddhist, the arising of shinjin which sees the foolish limitations of the ego and surrenders them to the nurturance of all-embracing Other Power.

Of course, there are many other things one could also do, and much to learn and explore if one wishes, but none of it really goes beyond fleshing out those bones which provide the support system for a Shin life.

All that one needs to do as a Shin Buddhist is take refuge and entrust one's self to the wisdom and compassion of Amida.

Beyond that, there is no need to do anything else.

Appreciating the Sutras

ANDREW COOPER, writing in the Buddhist magazine *Tricycle,* says that Western Buddhists tend to focus on commentarial literature rather than the sutras. I hadn't really thought about this, but he seems to be on to something.

I've spent a lot more time reading Shinran, Honen, and other Shin writers in recent years than I've spent reading the three Pure Land sutras. And of the three, the one I've read least in recent years is the *Larger Pure Land Sutra,* even though for Shinran it was *the* sutra which most embodied the Dharma. It's not that I'm ignorant of the Pure Land sutras—I've spent lots of time in previous years studying these texts—but somehow I'd fallen into trading the richness of the sutras for the clarity of the commentaries.

To rectify this, I started reading the *Larger Pure Land Sutra* again recently. And it blows my mind. Coming back to it after some time, I'm struck by the beauty and power of this text. The Buddha is so benevolent here, his relationship with Ananda is so friendly and intimate. As the sutra says, "all the senses of the World-Honored

One radiated joy, his entire body appeared serene and glorious, and his august countenance looked most majestic" as he contemplated Amida. Ananda was struck by this, and asked the Buddha to explain his vision. "With joy in my heart, I wish to hear the Dharma," he implored. It seems like the entirety of Buddhism is contained in this work, especially as it opens with an extensive portrayal of the bodhisattva path, concluding that the bodhisattva

> blocks the paths to the three evil realms, opens the gate of virtue, and, without waiting for their request, provides beings with the Dharma. He does this for the multitude of beings just as a dutiful son loves and respects his parents. He indeed looked upon sentient beings as his own self.

Reading the Forty-eight Vows is very, very moving. Going over the sutra, I wanted to get my wife to sit down with me so that we could enjoy this wonderful book together.

The vision which the Vows lays out is unrivaled: a desire to see a place where there is no racial discrimination, no war, no poverty, no hunger, no sexism, no pollution, only peace, cooperation, love, and wisdom. And in telling what the Buddha wants for us, we learn not only what the Pure Land provides but what is expected of us— to the extent that we are able—in this life here and now.

Nembutsu: Not for Parents

IN *Tannisho,* SHINRAN WRITES that he has never once said the nembutsu for the sake of his mother or father.

This is the sort of statement that is easily misunderstood if taken out of context: Didn't Shinran love his parents? What kind of ungrateful son was he? Was he purely selfish in his chanting? But I think these miss the point of Shinran's statement. With this subtle point, Shinran teaches us the true nature of the nembutsu, and in the process he teaches the true nature of parenthood as well.

Before Shinran's time, the nembutsu was always seen as *doing* something. People chanted nembutsu to ward off ghosts, or to make it rain, or to get Amida's attention so the Buddha would take them to the Pure Land. Often people chanted nembutsu for the sake of their parents—they believed that saying the nembutsu built up a store of good karma, which could be dedicated to their parents so they would be reborn in the Pure Land.

But Shinran changed how people thought about nembutsu. He taught that saying the nembutsu doesn't cause anything. Rather, the nembutsu expresses something that has already been *done:* Amida has already guaranteed that we will go to the Pure Land, so our nembutsu is an expression of joy and gratitude at this gift. This is the true nembutsu, the nembutsu of sincere thankfulness, according to Shinran. As I understand it, we don't need to say nembutsu for the sake of our parents, because Amida has already taken care of them.

Like Shinran, I don't say the nembutsu for the sake of my parents, but I do often say the nembutsu because of my parents. When I reflect on how much care and attention they have given me, as a child and even now as an adult, I am moved to say nembutsu. In the same passage, Shinran also points out that because we have been revolving in the wheel of life for countless eons, all creatures have been our mothers and fathers at some point. This is something amazing to think about. When I meditate on how all beings have been my parents, and that even now all beings and things together contribute to my life in so many unacknowledged ways, I feel deep gratitude toward everyone and everything. And I am grateful to Shinran for pointing out to me a way to express my thankful feelings, through *Namu Amida Butsu.*

The Dharma of Johnny Cash

'VE BEEN A FAN of Johnny Cash most my life, so I was interested to see the biopic *Walk the Line*. I thought they did a good job with it. One aspect which I felt should have received more attention was Johnny's religious feelings. Johnny Cash was a committed Christian of the best type, the kind who struggles with himself and his religion and lives it day to day, without trying to forcefully impose it on anyone else. He saw the dark side in himself that needed taming by a higher power, and for him it turned out to be Jesus.

I've never been a Christian and never been seriously tempted to go in that direction, but Johnny Cash's hard-won spirituality is one I can relate to deeply. Like Johnny I feel myself pulled in directions that I know I shouldn't, and I have to remind myself of the good things in my life that I jeopardize by giving in. When Johnny sings about "The Beast in Me," I'm right there with him, and I too "Walk the Line" because I'm aware of how my actions have consequences for those I love. And there's something so Shin about his conviction that "I'm Just an Old Lump of Coal, But I'm Gonna Be a Diamond Someday." That's the country evangelical version of Shinran's classic conviction that "we who are like bits of rubble will be turned into gold" by the power of the Primal Vow.

His religion isn't my religion—and yet, at the same time, it is.

Johnny Cash went back to the Pure Land a few years ago, and we're all poorer without him.

Dirty Jobs

THERE'S A SHOW on the Discovery Channel called *Dirty Jobs*. The premise is that the host goes around visiting people who have really dirty, smelly, messy jobs: plumbers, trash collectors, worm farmers, shark autopsy technicians, owl vomitologists, and so on. He hangs out with them, tries his hand at doing their job (usually poorly), and demonstrates vividly to us just how awful their jobs are. But the point isn't to feel glad that we don't have jobs as gross as theirs. The real point of *Dirty Jobs* is that thousands of people *are* working everyday at really undesirable jobs so that we can enjoy the relative comfort, hygiene, and convenience of modern life. The host wants us to acknowledge their sacrifices and feel thankful to them for enabling us to live in a way that isn't "dirty."

I really admire this show. Before I watched it, I didn't have a clear sense for how many factors must come together to allow me to live as well as I do. Sure, I saw the guys haul off the trash and recycling every week from behind my building, and every now and then I had to call a plumber for help. But all the while there were so many people I wasn't aware of who toiled in dirty jobs so that I could eat, enjoy my home, receive electricity, gas, and water, wear decent clothes, and basically do virtually anything and everything that I do.

This is yet another expression of interconnection, of inner togetherness. Interconnection means that I can have a clean job (being a professor) only because someone else has a dirty job (hauling away my trash) that supports me. Even if we aren't aware of it, what those people are doing affects us. Interconnection also means that even if we aren't aware of it, what we do impacts others too. Somehow, on some level, what I do affects the violence in the Middle East, the homeless people down on Skid Row, the migrants working in the fields, and everyone else. We all share this inner togetherness.

For me, an important part of Buddhism is waking up to the myriad ways in which I am interconnected with others. When shows like *Dirty Jobs* reveal to me my indebtedness, I feel humbled and thankful. Then, I try my best to act in ways that will make positive contributions to everyone who shares this inner togetherness with me, returning a small portion of that gift with compassion and gratitude.

Hitler's Buddha-Nature

A QUESTION CAME UP in the Thursday afternoon study class at the West Los Angeles Buddhist Temple, which I have heard other Buddhists ask before. Reverend Fumiaki Usuki mentioned the common Buddhist understanding that all beings have Buddha-nature. Someone then asked, "Did Hitler have Buddha-nature?"

At first this might seem like a clichéd question. But actually, it is vitally important. Could someone as evil as Adolf Hitler have Buddha-nature? Wasn't he obviously beyond the possibility of redemption, to say nothing of the potential to become a Buddha? The core of this question is even more important: are there some people whom Amida cannot or *will not* liberate from samsara? This question concerns the most central truths of Jodo Shinshu Buddhism.

Shinran is pretty explicit on this point. As he says in *Kyogyoshin-sho,* "Among all human beings and even insects that leap or worms that crawl, there is none that does not see Amida Buddha's light." All human beings, Hitler included. Even worms. That's about as clear as you could want it. Amida's light reaches all beings. That means Hitler, Osama bin Laden, Charles Manson, your least favorite politicians, your irritating co-worker, Bill O'Reilly, everybody. No matter how evil, deluded, or just plain annoying a person is, they are still within the reach of Amida's light. They may not perceive it now, but ultimately they will awaken to the way of the Buddha.

There's something else that Shinran said in *Kyogyoshinsho* that seems relevant to this question. "In their selfless love, these incarnated ones—Devadatta, Ajatasatru, Vaidehi—all aspired to save the multitudes of beings from pain and affliction, and in his compassion, Shakyamuni, the great hero, sought indeed to bless those committing the five grave offenses, those slandering the Dharma, and those lacking the seed of Buddhahood."

First, we see here that Shinran considered Devadatta (who tried to assassinate the Buddha) and Ajatasatru (who murdered his own father), two of the most evil persons in the Buddhist records, to be bodhisattvas in disguise. Their seemingly evil and certainly harmful acts led directly to Shakyamuni Buddha teaching the *Contemplation Sutra,* in which for the first time the idea that even a single utterance of nembutsu is sufficient is taught. I'm certainly *not* saying that Hitler was a bodhisattva, but sometimes someone who seems evil or bad to us may also end up being of some benefit, and that's worth keeping in mind. Secondly, Shinran's quote reveals that these teachings were designed to bless those who were hopelessly evil and even those who allegedly lacked Buddha-nature.

That's powerful stuff. Most religions divide humanity into two categories: those who can/will be saved and those who won't. This has led to tremendous suffering in human history. But for Shin Buddhists, there is only one category of people and it includes everyone: those who, like us, are foolish beings, yet who also, like us, will be awakened to buddhahood by Amida.

Amida's Emancipation
Proclamation

MY FAMILY COMES FROM TEXAS, a proudly unusual state that used to be its own separate country. Besides being the birthplace of the Lone Ranger, the Dallas Cowboys, and, yes, George W. Bush, Texas has its own cultural holidays. My favorite one has always been Juneteenth. Now when I think about it, Juneteenth seems to reflect the central liberating truths of Jodo Shinshu Buddhism.

Juneteenth celebrates the day when Texas' slaves learned that they had been freed. The Emancipation Proclamation legally set them free on January 1, 1863. However, for some reason the Texan slaveholders neglected to tell their slaves about this development—and so the slaves continued laboring and suffering for several more years. Finally, on June 19, 1865, an American general sailed into Galveston and announced that legal slavery had been abolished. Huge celebrations broke out among the freed slaves, and for over 140 years since there have been annual memorial observances commemorating this event, known nowadays as Juneteenth.

We're just like those poor men and women in Texas before they heard the announcement. They were free, but they didn't know it (worse still, weren't allowed to know it, just as there are whole industries devoted to preventing us from getting over our addictions and attachments). Then someone told them that they were free, that they had been free all along, and when they trusted this amazing proclamation they felt the bonds fall off and disappear. Just so, Amida's Vow—Buddha's Emancipation Proclamation—freed us long ago, but we don't realize it, and we continue to toil and suffer in the endless cycle of samsara. Then, one day we hear about Amida's actions on our behalf and entrust ourselves to Amida's compassion, and we are filled with awe and gratitude.

When we awaken to the operation of Other Power in our lives, nothing really changes. We don't *receive* freedom from our foolishness—we discover that this freedom already existed, but we just didn't know it. Amida was always embracing us and the Pure Land was always present, but we didn't realize it.

It's a cause for celebration just like that which broke out on Juneteenth all those years ago—as the *Larger Pure Land Sutra* says, we feel like leaping and dancing with joy. We celebrate by saying nembutsu, and from then on chanting reminds us of that unexpected gift of freedom.

In the Pot

ONCE HEARD A STORY that summed up the difference between the sagely path and the path of Pure Land.

Long ago, a rural village in Japan decided to build a temple and invite a Buddhist monk to come and minister to them. There were two applicants who seemed qualified, so the village decided to put them to a test in order to determine which one would be their new spiritual leader.

In the middle of the village two gigantic iron pots were set up and a fire was lit under each one, bringing the water inside to a boil. Then the two applicants were asked what they would do with the pots to prove their worthiness. The first monk was an advanced tantric meditator. Without batting an eye, he calmly climbed into the first pot, which reached up to his neck. Unaffected by the boiling water, the monk meditated for hours. The villagers were amazed and impressed—here was a monk who truly had amazing powers.

The second applicant was a Shin priest. He didn't have impressive robes like the tantric monk, and he didn't even shave his head.

Everyone wondered how he could possibly do better than the first man, especially since while the tantric monk had been quietly preparing himself for his intense meditation, the Shin priest had just been chatting casually with the villagers, asking about their families and how the harvest was going. But when his turn came, the Shin priest gave a big smile and walked up to the second boiling pot.

"Quick!" he called out. "Bring me some vegetables and salt!" Puzzled, the villagers gave him what he requested. Whistling to himself, the Shin priest chopped up the veggies and threw them in the pot with the salt. After a while he called out, "Soup's ready!" He served the whole village supper from the big pot, and talked with them late into the night about their hopes and fears, offering advice and telling them to take comfort in Amida's never-abandoning compassion.

In the morning, the villagers thanked the tantric monk for coming and asked the Shin priest to stay and minister to their village.

Namu Death

NOT LONG AGO my Grandpa died, and shortly thereafter my great aunt Eula Belle passed away. She was the baby in the family—in fact, she was often just called "Aunt Baby"—though she was already in her nineties when she died. But she had three older siblings, so even at her advanced age she still couldn't escape being Aunt Baby. Her siblings—my grandmother, my great aunt Mineola, and my great uncle Brother (a nickname he'd earned by being the only boy in his family)—all died within the last few years. Their deaths bring to a close an epic chapter in the history of my father's family, and leave me without some of the most important touchstones of my life and identity. I am saddened by the loss of these family giants. And yet, as I reflect on the situation, I find that I am moved to gratitude for the fact of death in the midst of the wonder of life.

Shakyamuni Buddha identified death as one of the four great causes of suffering in the world. The others are sickness, old age, and in fact birth itself, since it leads to the pains we experience in life. I'm certainly not going to argue with the Buddha—death is a cause of great misery. Among those left behind, we feel bereft and broken, and are often financially or otherwise imperiled by the death of another. For the dead, the process of dying itself is often tremendously hard, both physically and psychologically, as our primal animal self-attachment usually refuses to give up life, dragging out the inevitable. And for all of us, the worry of death—our own and that of those we care for—can loom ominously over this already often difficult life.

But there is another side to death as well. We could not enjoy life without death—life exists only because of death. All living things survive on the death of countless others: from the animals consumed for meat to the plants that push their roots deep into the soil that has been fertilized by the decomposed beings that came before. Death is the necessary ingredient that sustains life, recycling precious nutrients and making room for new generations.

As much as I miss them, the elder generation of my family enjoyed more than 450 years of life collectively, and had they continued indefinitely it would have removed scarce resources from the mouths of the young. So too, when it is my time to go to the Pure Land, I hope to die well and clear some space for the fresh ones coming behind me. After all, I am only borrowing life's resources for a time.

So somehow when I say "Namu Amida Butsu" out of gratitude for all I receive, I have to include thankfulness for death along with thankfulness for life—otherwise, my gratitude is incomplete.

Namu life, namu death, namu *all* that sustains me and everything that lives and dies.

Thanksgiving Service

A COUPLE OF YEARS AGO, I spent Thanksgiving with my wife's family in Georgia. I have always thought of Thanksgiving as the most Shin of all holidays: not only does it celebrate family and community, it is specifically based on the idea of recognizing our indebtedness and expressing gratitude for the things we receive. Surely this is the heart of Shin Buddhism. Whether you are saying the nembutsu at temple or counting your blessings over a shared turkey dinner, the attitude of thanksgiving is what it's all about.

Thinking back on our Thanksgiving holidays in Georgia, it is the time with family that most stands out. Gathering with the family also means that many generations come together in one place. In the past, it was common for multiple generations to live in one household or at least one town or village. But today we often live separated from much of our family, and these holidays take on extra meaning because children, parents, and grandparents can be with one another. Family is the most natural place for us to learn about indebtedness: even if we can't see the more abstract ways in which all people and things contribute to our lives, we can at least acknowledge the direct effect of parents and ancestors in bringing us into the world and raising us. The separation of family members in the modern world is surely part of the difficulty we have in developing thankful hearts.

When families gather, little dramas naturally play out as well. One of my wife's sisters was only seven years old, so she was still learning about manners and the way the world works (of course, I in my thirties am also still learning these things). One big problem she had was with saying "Thank you." When she received a present, she was obviously happy, but she had a hard time actually thanking people. It wasn't clear whether this was because of embarrassment, greed, forgetfulness, or any of a host of other causes. Nonetheless, she got in trouble at one point and was sent to her room—followed by a lecture on thankfulness by her parents.

This incident got me thinking. How do we understand lack of gratitude in reference to Shin Buddhism? We often talk about how we need to be thankful to Amida and that it is the heart of entrusting, the grateful heart, that leads to our birth in the Pure Land. If my wife's sister never learns to be grateful, will she be forever shut out of the Pure Land?

In my understanding, even an ungrateful person will be born in the Pure Land. Amida accepts us just as we are, even when we don't accept ourselves or others find us unacceptable. As Shinran taught, Amida knows us as persons deeply sunk in delusion and attachment, yet allows us to ride on the power of the Primal Vow all the same. Shinran affirmed that even murderers will be accepted into the Pure Land, so surely the ungrateful will be too.

Even so, this doesn't take away the necessity for gratitude.

Let us look again, carefully, at the situation of the little girl, who in a way also stands for all us too: She is ungrateful, but nevertheless she is embraced by great compassion. Other Power works to awaken her, through the voice of her parents, teachers, and friends. She will not be abandoned. But while she persists in being ungrateful, she is harming herself. Stuck in a self-centered mindset that greedily wants things but doesn't want to acknowledge the source of her benefit, she is closed-off from the very human connections that seek to share love and happiness with her. She thinks of herself as a solitary unit, missing the joy of her interconnection with others. Her refusal to say thank you hurts the feelings of people who care for her, and worries those entrusted to be her guides. She is only able to enjoy one half of her presents: the things themselves. She cannot enjoy the other, better half: the joy of the receiving itself, which is only felt to its utmost by the open heart of thankfulness. In short, her life is worse off because she cannot manifest a grateful heart.

And it's so easy for us to deprive ourselves of the joys of our lives in the same way.

The greatest gift of Shin, and of our own true and real life, is only touched when we wake up to our fundamental indebtedness and learn to live a life that makes every day Thanksgiving.

Just As We Are

REMEMBER one Thanksgiving service that was conducted at the West Los Angeles Buddhist Temple. The sermon touched on some essential points of Shin Buddhism that I think may not be conveyed too well to people who only read Shinran and don't have contact with the living tradition of Jodo Shinshu. Here are some of the main points Reverend Fumiaki Usuki made:

1. Form and ritual are good, but warmth, flexibility, and easygoingness are more important

2. Being familiar with the letter of the teachings is good, but the implicit meaning is more important

3. Saying nembutsu is good, but the mind of gratitude—be it toward Amida, parents, or the Thanksgiving Day turkey that feeds us—is more important

The facilitator for the service was a new, Caucasian member who didn't know how to say any of the Japanese words. She made many mistakes, but no one minded and her efforts were met with welcoming applause at the end.

In a way, I think that was the most important moment of the whole service, as people just accepted her for who she was and appreciated the offering she made—not getting caught up in the offering they wished she made or thought she should make.

What a gift!

Death Wish

S ENATOR TIM JOHNSON of South Dakota had to have emergency brain surgery in 2006, near Christmastime. If Johnson, a Democrat, had died or had to resign, the Republican governor of South Dakota would have appointed a Republican to take his place, and just like that the Republicans would have snatched the Senate back from the Democrats who had won it in the November election.

Although I am not affiliated with either party, I was displeased with how the Republicans ran the country when they controlled the White House and Congress. So I was glad to see the Democrats gain Congress and offer some balance to our government. I hoped this would lead to a resolution of the Iraq quagmire, bring more compassion and sense back to our domestic policies, and less corruption. That's not really the point here, however. What I really want to talk about is how difficult it is for us to really be good in the way that the Buddha asks of us. Senator Johnson's situation reminded me of this point, which is central to Shinran's thought.

What if the situation had been reversed? If Johnson had been a Republican with a Democratic governor, and his death would have been the key to usher in a Democratic Senate, how would I have felt?

As much as I wish to deny it, I believe that in my heart I would have hoped for Johnson to die from a brain hemorrhage.

This is really a terrible fact about human nature. Even though people suffer and die because of bad policies, that really doesn't excuse the desire for a man to drop dead and leave his family traumatized just before Christmas. I am sure many Republicans hoped for just that outcome, even if they wouldn't admit it to others—or even to themselves.

But how can I blame them? Although this is an awful way to be, I too am like this. As, I believe, are most people.

No matter how much meditation or chanting or other practices you do, one's first reaction in such situations is probably always going to be for self-benefit. The Buddha wanted us to purify our hearts and learn to look with compassion and equanimity toward all people, friends and enemies. It is a beautiful goal and one we should strive for, but we fool ourselves if we think we can *fully* achieve it. We can move from more bad to less bad, but as Shinran puts it, we will never really know good in the way that Amida knows good.

That gap between our best effort toward goodness and real goodness is not small. And ultimately it is not within our power to bridge this gap. When I encounter that chasm between the good person that I want to be, and the foolish being I really am (and always will be), I am moved to say, "Namu Amida Butsu." It is a nembutsu of regret and apology, of acknowledgment of how life is, but also still of gratitude—because while Buddhism urges me to be the best I can be toward others, it doesn't demand that I do the impossible, and we are never rejected for falling short. When our efforts do fail, Amida nonetheless embraces us. In Other Power there is never abandonment.

And strange as it may sound, at these times it is also a nembutsu of gratitude precisely for being less than perfect. If I were someone truly and perhaps uniquely able to overcome my self-interest and think only of others, then I would be cut off from the rest of humanity, who cannot achieve this Herculean task. Being imperfect keeps me on a level with everyone else, and means that we can all enter the Pure Land together with one another.

Even if I don't agree with the Republicans (or many Democrats, for that matter), I don't want to enjoy happiness while they suffer. I will only be happy when all of us fellow deluded beings can be at peace and awaken as one. So for the ultimate reconciliation of all beings in the Pure Land, I say "Namu Amida Butsu" in thanks.

Transformed

A T THE NEW YORK BUDDHIST CHURCH there are all sorts of fascinating people who have come to the Dharma. Although commitment to Pure Land Buddhism holds them together, many also enjoy learning about other forms of Buddhism as well. One member of the temple, Dimitri, has for many years studied the scriptures of the Theravada school, the oldest surviving form of Buddhism. Since part of the Shin approach is respect and admiration toward other forms of Buddhism, Dimitri is often encouraged to share his knowledge.

I remember one study session we had that Tai Unno led. We were discussing the Buddhist doctrine of the *kleshas,* the defilements or mental conditioning and attachments that prevent human beings from acting in enlightened ways. Often it is said that awakening grows out of the defilements and the gritty stuff of the everyday world, like a beautiful lotus whose seed is deep in the muck, yet whose flower reaches up above the mud and dirty water to blossom in the sun. Dimitri said that in the Theravada view they say, "I am not the muck." In the Mahayana view, they say "I am in the muck, but I get out of it." In the Vajrayana Buddhist tradition they say, "I am the muck."

Dr. Unno looked thoughtful and said, "That is very interesting. It is rather like our own Shin Buddhism. We say: 'I am the muck— but the muck is transformed.'"

Wonder-Struck

THERE IS A BEAUTIFUL TERM that appears in the *Contemplation of Amida Sutra*. According to the text, when Shakyamuni Buddha revealed the presence of the Pure Land and that all one had to do to go there was to call Amida's name, Queen Vaidehi was "wonder-struck." What a lyrical way to express our first amazement at encountering the Primal Vow and the great compassion of Other Power. Truly, there is something wondrous and striking about the discovery that Amida offers us freedom and ease despite all our shortcomings.

There are many things in my life that fill me with wonder and awe. Sometimes it is the beauty of nature when I'm out hiking in Topanga Canyon or Will Rogers State Park. The scenery is breathtaking and the harmony of the natural world just beyond the crazy chaotic city is humbling—it's easy to understand why Shakyamuni uses descriptions of lovely trees, streams, and birds to evoke the Pure Land for Vaidehi. Other times people I know or read about strike me with wonder, when I learn about the hardships they've managed to overcome or the good things they've done for one another. Although this is a difficult world with many problems, there are many people who try to make it a better place for us to live in. And sometimes wonder strikes me just at the realization that I am alive and breathing, and that my life is upheld by the uncountable actions of so many people, beings, and things. The whole world comes together to enable our lives in each moment—surely this is some sort of miracle.

Whenever I wake up for a moment to the infinite support of others, I feel "wonder-struck." Like Vaidehi, suffering in her prison, I feel suddenly released for a moment from my problems and given a glimpse of true and real life. Without a thought, "Namu Amida Butsu" pops out. Even in the toil of our daily routines, life offers us many opportunities to wonder and give thanks.

I hope that we can all remain open to the call of Amida in each moment of wonder—may it strike us often!

Permanent Defeat

N THE FIRST PAGE OF *The Old Man and the Sea,* Ernest Hemingway describes how the tattered sail of the fisherman looked like "the flag of permanent defeat." That's an evocative phrase that has stayed with me long after I finished reading the book. In some ways, I think it applies to Jodo Shinshu Buddhism.

To me, the stoles that we wear in the worship hall (called *kesas*) are our flags of permanent defeat. When you slip the stole over your head and go before Amida Buddha, you are acknowledging that your own power is never enough to get by. You are permanently defeated. Even the stole itself seems to signal this defeat. Once upon a time the stole was the full robe worn by Buddha's disciples, who were celibate monks and nuns striving mightily to free themselves from samsara. But over time the robe has shrunk until it is just this little strip of cloth, incapable of protecting us from the elements or hiding our nakedness. From holy monks we have devolved into ordinary foolish laypeople, fully exposed for what we are.

And yet, it is at the moment of permanent defeat that we are enabled to "win" our liberation. When we truly give up on trying futilely to become Buddha through our own limited efforts, we discover that Buddha has always been embracing us. It is like the fisherman in Hemingway's story. He hoisted the flag of permanent defeat, even as he set out once again to wrestle a living from the sea. That very sail, tattered and defeated, carried him out to the deep ocean waters, where great fishes silently swim. With the wind, the sail, the waters, and everything coming together, he was able to hook a fish and fulfill his destiny as a fisherman. He still put in his share of the work, yet his efforts were only fruitful because of all the other factors that allowed his efforts to succeed.

Jodo Shinshu is the Buddhism of permanent defeat. That isn't something to celebrate or take pride in. We are only special in the way we have come to realize that we aren't going to reach the goal on our own, that our defeat is permanent, part of our nature, and existed before we even tried. Yet it is by accepting the permanency of our defeat that we become aware of another avenue to the finish line, of the possibility that, odd as it may seem at first, defeat leads to victory when it causes us to relax back into our natural state and simply let Other Power, like the calm but relentless winds and tides, carry us to our destination.

And when surrender has been declared, strangely enough, we are enabled to go forward and live our lives as Buddhists in gratitude, seeking to do good and walk the path—without concerns of winning or losing.

Bittersweet Buddhism

For me, the word "bittersweet" really captures my Shin Buddhism. Buddhism for me is life itself, and that life is surely bittersweet. We are foolish beings, incapable of achieving what we want. We hurt, we suffer, we age, we die. We fail to bring others the happiness we wish for them. Mired in my ego, lost in my own stupid delusions, the nembutsu is the only thing that is true and real, like a buoy that a sailor clings to in a raging sea.

Yet life is so sweet, so incredible. It amazes me, simply amazes me that I am alive. Every day I get to breathe, think, love, enjoy the sunshine, learn, and say the nembutsu. There is too much joy for me to bear, I have to say nembutsu or I will burst. Nembutsu is the only safety valve for the sweetness of life that is always threatening to overwhelm me.

I say nembutsu both because I feel great sadness and great joy. It is nembutsu of the bitterness of life and the sweetness of life. And bitterness and sweetness aren't really two—I only know the sweetness in comparison with the bitterness.

The bitterness provokes my gratitude at being enabled to feel sweet joy and love, even in such an imperfect, disappointing world.

Awakening the Buddha
Without

THE LATE 1990S brought us a boom in Buddhist publishing, some of which made it onto the lists of bestselling books. One of the most successful was Lama Surya Das's *Awakening the Buddha Within.* It's a very readable, simple approach to Buddhism.

I'm bringing attention to this book as much for the title as anything else. The idea of "awakening the Buddha within" is a basic tenet of most Buddhist converts in America. Partially through ideas that have their original root in Scottish Common Sense philosophy (exemplified by thinkers like Thomas Reid and William Hamilton, this eighteenth- and nineteenth-century school was an enormous influence on American culture, especially Protestant Christianity), partially through New Age concepts, and partially through ideas genuinely held by some forms of Buddhism, there has developed an attitude that somewhere inside of us lurks a Buddha who constitutes our true essence. Here is how Surya Das puts it on page 16 of his book:

When you genuinely become you, a Buddha realizes Buddhahood. You become a Buddha by actualizing your own original innate nature. This nature is primordially pure. This is your true nature, your natural mind. This innate Buddha-nature doesn't need to achieve enlightenment because it is always already perfect, from the beginningless beginning. We only have to awaken to it. There is nothing more to seek or look for.

This is an appealing vision, and there was a time when I accepted it uncritically. This view is flattering; it is hopeful; it is enticing. But I worry that it can lead to misunderstandings of core Buddhist principles.

My understanding of Buddhism is based in shunyata, often translated as "emptiness." Shunyata is the phenomenon of *lack:* we lack any "original" nature, any "innate" nature, any "true" nature— heck, any "nature" at all. All things are selfless, built of composite parts that come together temporarily and later disperse. There is no Buddha hiding inside somewhere waiting for the other parts to get out of the way.

Surya Das and others who talk about innate buddhahood sometimes have sophisticated understandings which are able to harmonize the conflicting concepts of shunyata, impermanence, selflessness, and "innate nature." Often, however, many convert Buddhists take up rhetoric about primordial pureness and use it as an ego-building device. The concept of "the Buddha within," taken on the conventional level that most people I've seen do, reinforces egoism and acts as a fundamental obstacle to understanding the truth of shunyata. Yet it is through seeing shunyata that buddhas are born—it is the apprehension of vast emptiness, total interconnection, absolute selflessness, and constant change which accords with the way things really are.

Not all fall into the trap of misappropriating this idea of "the Buddha within," of course. But for those who do, perhaps a corrective can be offered in turning to awaken to "the Buddha *without*." Rather than focusing on a nonexistent personal core buried somewhere in the body or mind or spirit, it would be more useful to turn the gaze outward and observe the "buddhaness" of all things. All awakening takes place through the ceaseless support of the entire universe, not simply through one's "own" efforts. The meditator in his cave, the sutra scholar in her study, the bodhisattvas with their sleeves rolled up—all are enabled to do what they do through the natural working of Dharma, of the entirety of the universe itself. No buddha has ever awoken in isolation. Human beings wake up to reality because others provide food and clothing, shelter and safety, direct teachings and life lessons, models good and bad. In a way, Shakyamuni only became the Buddha because one day he was walking in the city and someone helped him out by having died. Another man helped him by being sick, and another by being poor. He became the Buddha because his family had nurtured him through childhood, bees had pollinated the crops that provided his sustenance, and the monsoons had brought rain each year. Mara the Deceiver lent a hand by confronting and challenging the former prince, while the Bodhi Tree provided strength and shelter.

Too often our depictions of enlightenment are individualistic, and our stories of how buddhas come to be focus on single persons as great heroes of the Dharma. But, to adapt a well-known African saying, it takes a village to grow a buddha. "The Buddha without" is constantly working to bring about our awakening, even as we flounder in the depths of human foolishness which far more closely approximates any "true nature" than idealized visions of Buddhas within.

I don't mean to say that Surya Das and others are necessarily wrong. Seeking the Buddha within can lead some to awakening, though it is a hard road. My concern is that this path is so frequently misconstrued, and that Americans don't need stories that inspire confidence so much as ones that engender humility. Americanism is a cult of individuality, and a dangerous one at that. Turning to the Buddha without as our focus can help diminish that ingrained cultural egoism and lead to a more balanced awakening that locates the Buddha not inside, but in all.

When shunyata is realized, we see that our fundamental nature is not one of inner buddhaness, but of an existence which is completely relational in nature. Thus observing the relations that underlie our practice is a powerful tool for waking up to who and how we really are, one which "de-centers" the inherent pitfall of self-orientation contained in the quest for inner buddhas.

Shin Conflict Resolution

CONFLICT IS UNAVOIDABLE in life, and when it arises in my own life, I try my best to apply Buddhist principles to help ease the potential suffering of conflict. Even though I apply my understanding every day, it can be hard to articulate a specifically Shin approach to conflict resolution—because so much of Shin Buddhism has to do with feelings rather than abstract philosophy. That makes it hard to put into words, even when one has a pretty good idea of what one wants to say. Luckily, we have a very articulate and thoughtful example in Reverend Taitetsu Unno, who has often been able to say or demonstrate what the rest of us can't seem to get across. Here is an example of Reverend Unno's straightforward articulation of the Dharma. He puts into simple words my own thoughts better than I could do myself:

What is the secret of creating a strong [Sangha]? The answer is simple—by applying the Shin teachings to all its deliberations. What does this mean? It means to apply the teachings to work together and to resolve any disagreements. This involves two points: (1) recognize that the source of conflicts is never the "other" but one's own ego-self, and (2) manifest the strength and wisdom provided by the Dharma to deal with one's own subjective biases and thus become more open to other people's views, regardless of agreement or disagreement.

This is very hard to do in real life, which is why it's sort of funny that Pure Land is called "the easy path." But the power of the Primal Vow does give us that push to "drive all blames into one," as the Kagyu Tibetan Buddhists say. When we first look to see how we have helped to create a bad situation, rather than first looking at others as troublemakers, we can often see that we are a primary source of the problem.

I can't say that I succeed in living my life this way all the time, but it is the basic perspective which I try to bring to my day.

Grateful for Suffering?

A FRIEND OF MINE asked the provocative question of whether we can be grateful for the things we undeservedly suffer from, yet which contribute to our awakening. This is an issue that Buddhists have struggled with for a long time. The ancient Indian Buddhist scholar Shantideva, for instance, expressed joyful gratitude to people who harmed him because they helped him along the Dharma path.

I can't pretend to have equanimity equal to Shantideva's, but I do see his point. The slings and arrows I've experienced are an important part of the process that has taken me to where I am today. I won't bore you with a catalog of my woes, but certainly there are things I've suffered that I had no direct hand in causing: sometimes you're the skunk who happens to cross the road just as the big truck races by. But I don't believe that this is an unjust universe—nor that it is a just one. In every life there is both justice and injustice, though their ratio can fluctuate quite a bit.

I'll add a note here that in many cases it has been my own unjust actions, when I caused harm to someone who didn't deserve it, that have been my concern. I gave up on the strong-willed bodhisattva ideal after I discovered that I could never be sure that my actions really benefited anyone in the long run, and that my wisdom was insufficient to prevent me from harming others even when my intentions were sincere. Even as a Zen practitioner committed to carrying out the bodhisattva way, a person dedicated to fulfilling the precepts comprehensively, I was often a vehicle for injustice to others, both loved ones and strangers, despite my best efforts.

Now I entrust my awakening process to Amida, a higher wisdom and compassion than my own limited light. I haven't given up on the bodhisattva ideal of cherishing and helping others, but I'm not fooling myself anymore that I might be making substantive progress on that ideal. Illuminated by the light of Other Power, I still sometimes serve as a vehicle for injustice. That's what it means to live in an impossibly interconnected universe, where injustice is a fact of life: you're never going to escape injustice—the injustice you suffer and the injustice you perpetrate—because there is nowhere to escape to and no action unconnected to both structures and random acts of injustice.

Even in the Pure Land you don't escape injustice, because your buddhahood moves you to return to the suffering world immediately to heed the cries of the afflicted. Becoming a buddha is just going to make you completely aware of injustice, not immune from it—though I do imagine buddhas can perhaps handle it a lot better than I can now.

He with Horns Is Self

ASAHARA SAICHI is one of the most famous myokonin, the joyous untutored simple people who in a way serve as the Shin counterpart to Zen masters. In 1919 a portrait was painted of Saichi. He insisted that the painter include a pair of horns on his head, to symbolize his "devil's heart."

Reverend Umeda Kenkyo, a famous Shin priest and scholar, wrote a verse on the picture, that goes in part:

> He with horns is Self, he with prayerful hands is Dharma;
> Dharma, fully embracing Self, softens the deeds of body,
> mouth, and mind. With the cause of the flaming wheel of
> desire extinguished, the ambrosial heart is replete...

It's an inspiring image: imagine what it would be like if we actually somehow did have horns on our head or maybe wore some sort of headgear to simulate horns. Every day we would be reminded of the Mara-nature within, lurking in ourselves and in all we meet.

Because we don't have such horns, it is easy for us to imagine that we are good, or even if we are down on ourselves, to imagine that other people are good.

Reverend Umeda points out that we with horns—visible or otherwise—are embraced by the Dharma. But while it may apply to Saichi, I can't apply the rest of his verse to myself. Every day I am crushed by the flaming wheel of desire, and every day I say the nembutsu thinking that maybe tomorrow I won't be crushed. But it always happens. I was crushed yesterday, and I was crushed today. And flaming desire will surely crush me tomorrow, just as surely as somewhere in my mind I'll imagine that it won't.

It's so hard to give up self-power, even as little as the thought "I'll just say the nembutsu and entrust Amida, then maybe I won't be crushed tomorrow." But it ain't gonna happen that way. Dharma may soften deeds of body, speech, and mind, but it doesn't completely eliminate them, and as long as we are alive, those horns are going to be there. Intoning nembutsu or with mouth closed tight, the wheel just keeps rolling back and forth over me.

Luckily, Amida doesn't abandon the crushed, even if they don't perceive the wheel on their backs, even if they feel the heat and weight and say "I bet *this one* is really the very last time I'll be crushed!"

Sinking into the Vow

'VE NOTICED THAT over time my relationship to the nembutsu has changed. In fact, the nembutsu I use has itself changed somewhat.

There are a number of Japanese variations on the nembutsu. Shinran preferred the ten-character "Kimyo Jinjippo Mugeko Nyorai." Rennyo preferred the six-character "Namu Amida Butsu," which is now the standard rendition of the nembutsu.

When I first began to move into the Other Power path, I was chanting "Namu Kuan Yin Pusa" ("I take refuge in Kuan-Yin Bodhisattva"). Kuan-Yin Bodhisattva, the bodhisattva of compassion, is one of the three primary Pure Land figures, along with Amida Buddha and Daiseishi Bodhisattva, who represents perfect wisdom. It was Kuan-Yin who initially came to my rescue after I'd lost my faith in Zen. I remember many nights walking the streets of New York, mile after mile, hour after hour, softly chanting a syllable of the Kuan-Yin nembutsu with each step, wondering what was happening to me and where I was being led. Eventually, fortunately,

I ended up at New York Buddhist Church and the American Buddhist Study Center, and began to learn about Shin Buddhism in greater depth.

After my focus began to move from Amida's helper to Amida directly, I found that I preferred "Kimyo Jinjippo Mugeko Nyorai," like Shinran did. I always opened my devotions at home before the butsudan with this nembutsu. It still has a lot of appeal to me: there's something wonderfully spacious about the ten-character nembutsu that no other version quite captures for me.

Yet I eventually found my focus shifting once again, as I took up the common six-character nembutsu, "Namu Amida Butsu," and reveled in its directness. More than the ten character nembutsu, it has the quality of thanksgiving that is central to my understanding of the Pure Land way. Also, it is the most adaptable one to the several different tonal styles applied at temples, either the two-tone version we used at New York Buddhist Church or the four-tone version common at Chinese temples.

But now, without my being conscious of it, my nembutsu has shifted one more time. I realized the other day that I mainly say "Namandabu" now, not the formal "Namu Amida Butsu." All the time I catch this simple "namandabu, namandabu, namandabu" spilling out of me. I say it in the shower, walking from the bus, in bed at night, when I wake up, and many times throughout the day. Often, I don't even know I'm saying it until I have a moment of "Oh!" and catch myself after I've been uttering "namandabu" without really being fully aware of it. Other times, I'm just walking along happy that things are naturally just as they are and that "namandabu" just starts itself up, carrying me along.

This "namandabu" isn't really "I take refuge in Amida Buddha." To me, that's what the formal six-character Namu Amida Butsu does. "Namandabu" is really just "Thank you, thank you," or maybe even "My heart and Amida are one," if that makes any sense.

There's no striving, just a simple floating on the ocean of the Primal Vow.

"Namandabu, namandabu, namandabu." It's as natural as breathing. I can't put it any other way.

Trustingly We Cry

THE FIRST NOBLE TRUTH of Buddhism essentially states that this is a hard life that we all lead. Until we are fully awakened, there is always some measure of pain, dissatisfaction, restlessness, and suffering. Even the best of lives is touched at times by suffering; for many, suffering is a daily reality, not an abstraction. This recognition is called "noble" not because it is noble to suffer, but because there is nobility in truly facing up to the fundamental fact of imperfection in our lives.

But this starting point for Buddhism is also often misunderstood. The Buddha never said "life *is* suffering." He said that life *contains* suffering. It is neither all suffering nor all happiness, all good or all bad. Even in the times when we feel lowest, and however many setbacks we encounter, Other Power is always operating in our lives. For as long as we live, no matter what our circumstances, we are floating on the ocean of grace. The truth of emptiness means that today will pass and tomorrow will be different, that things are always in the process of becoming and we can have a hand in shaping them for the better.

Reverend Ernest Hunt, one of the first Caucasians to become a Shin Buddhist, wrote a hymn that expresses the joy Amida provides even as we acknowledge the pain of ourselves and others. It is sung frequently in our temples even today. Here are the first two sections:

When life is fair and sunlight gilds the day
When fortune smiles, and flowers adorn our way
Oft let us pause with grateful hearts to say
Namu Amida Butsu.

Even though our way leads 'neath a darkened sky
And to our loved ones pain and death draw nigh
Our tears may flow, yet trustingly we cry
Namu Amida Butsu.

Sometimes in this life, we say the nembutsu while smiling. Sometimes we say the nembutsu while crying. It is always the same nembutsu. The trusting heart is a gift that sustains us through the darkest paths of life, and gives us joy when we pause in gratitude and acknowledge the support of Other Power, never abandoning us and always drawing us on toward the Realm of Bliss.

I have known many people who have appreciated such support in their lives. People struggling with terminal illnesses, with severe disfigurements, with the loss of parents, spouses, and children, people facing financial problems beyond their means, and so many others. The nembutsu is not magic—it can't make these real problems go away.

But even as the tears flow, the cry of the heart that breaks and the cry of the heart that trusts mingle and are held fiercely by great compassion.

Buddhism, Addiction, and Twelve Steps

NOT LONG AGO I was asked by someone for help. This person is a drug addict struggling to stay clean. She's currently involved with Narcotics Anonymous (NA). The problem is that she has become a Buddhist, and the language and concepts of NA as usually understood don't seem to work very well with Buddhism. Her sponsor felt that she wasn't sufficiently answering a series of questions, and she was seeking a Buddhist answer to what she was being told she had to do. Privately, I wasn't sure that Buddhism and her twelve-step program, which follows from quite obvious evangelical Christian roots, were compatible. But she also said that she needed to stay in NA, that she was worried about committing suicide or being the victim of a violent crime if she didn't manage to get clean, and she didn't have access to other options.

A close family member also had some experience with NA, and I know through him and friends that addicts pretty much can't do things alone, they do need a group of this sort if they're going to avoid the very real dangers associated with drug addiction.

Therefore I did my best to answer the questions that had been posed to her, in a way that reflected my Buddhist understanding but also would hopefully satisfy her sponsor.

It was tough: Higher Power, insanity, restoration, coincidence—these aren't the currency of my Buddhism, and I had to work hard to translate my ideas into this language. I don't know if I was successful. But because this was a situation of real need, and because other people might find themselves in the same situation at some point, I wanted to share my responses to her questions. Maybe something I wrote will strike a chord, or maybe you'll disagree and think of a better way to answer if you find yourself in this sort of situation:

What does "trust the process" mean to you?

For me, trusting the process means putting my faith in the Buddha's prediction that all beings will achieve liberation. It also means trusting other people who have gone before me and described their processes: if wiser people than me have shown how NA or other programs can really work, then I'd be smart to pay attention and follow through, even when I hit bumps and things for the moment don't seem to be progressing.

What is hope?

For me, hope arises from the insight into emptiness. Emptiness doesn't mean that nothing exists, rather one meaning is that everything has the potential to change. Every situation, from my natural weaknesses to the state of the economy to the bloodiest of wars is empty and liable to change, so that I can count on things being different someplace down the road. This is especially true if I can find productive ways to work on influencing emptiness toward positive outcomes. Emptiness is great potentiality.

Do you have hope?

I do have hope, even though I'm a bit cynical in my views on many things. Part of what gives me hope is that I have seen people get better. In a recovery situation, I've seen some of my friends go from rock-bottom to happy, productive lives. This includes people who were in awful situations, and even people on whom everyone had given up as hopeless or even worthless. Emptiness means all bets are off and even the lowest of the low can become the highest of the high.

Define honesty, open-mindedness, and willingness.

These seem like core Buddhist values to me. Honesty means admitting when you're wrong or too weak to be stronger, and just letting that less than perfect fact of human existence sit there while you do your best. It also means not pretending to be something you aren't, which in a recovery situation includes not passing yourself off as doing better if you aren't really. It means telling the truth as much as you are able, and admitting to yourself at least when you haven't been entirely honest with others.

Open-mindedness means listening to other people's opinions and thoughts, including ones about yourself and your progress that you're not initially ready to accept. It means continuing to engage the program even when it seems like you're not getting anywhere, or when you think you don't have what it takes to get better.

Willingness means being open to change, and it means trying to move ahead even when you can't see the light at the end of the tunnel.

What does insanity mean to you?

Insanity is really the baseline state of the sentient being—we're all blinded by attachment to an illusory ego and craving, anger, and delusion toward the outer world. Only buddhas are fully sane. So it means giving up the idea that everything I think is right and that I truly understand the way the world works. In a recovery situation, it also speaks of the gradations of insanity—we may all be crazy from the Buddha's point of view, but if we cloud our minds further with intoxicants or submit endlessly to harmful impulses, we're piling insanity on top of insanity.

What does restoration mean to you?

Here's a really Christian concept that throws a monkey-wrench in the works. But if I'm going to be imaginative and try to work with the program, restoration to me means coming back to myself, becoming aware of my faults and my strengths, and working to do the best I can with what I am. True restoration would be to realize the suchness of the Dharmakaya; for a less exalted goal, I'd say that restoration would mean recapturing the level of independence and clarity that I've enjoyed at the best times of my life.

Write about your higher power.

For me, my higher power is Amida Buddha. This is the Buddha of Boundless Compassion and Wisdom, symbolized as life and light. After Shakyamuni, Amida is the most popular and most prayed-to Buddha, and the practice of calling upon Amida is perhaps the most widely spread Buddhist practice after taking refuge and precepts. Amida represents the totality of all the things that interdependently come together to produce my life and awakening. From a certain standpoint, you can say that Amida is the ultimate nature of the universe, or the awareness of the fully awakened mind. Amida isn't really a person, it's just that for the deluded sentient being symbols and potent myths are often necessary tools for navigating toward freedom. Ultimately, Amida is Buddha-nature: your own and that of all things.

What is the spiritual principle behind this step (relying on a higher power)?

As I understand it, the reliance on a higher power helps break down the attachment to the false self, by redirecting one's attention from the darkness of one's own mind toward the light of true consciousness. It cuts off the endless cycle of depression and self-obsession, and allows hope to blossom.

Look for evidence of a higher power, especially coincidences.

Here I can't quite go where your sponsor wants. I don't believe there is spiritual value in coincidences—to me that is superstition. This is because I don't believe supernatural forces *intervene* in our lives. In my view, there is no need for supernatural miracles. The evidence of Amida's presence is as simple as reflecting on the contingent circumstances that have produced me, and remembering all the love and care that have been put into sustaining my life by so many people, family, teachers, friends, even strangers I'll never know about.

Once you awaken to the vast network of support that each of us enjoys at every moment—the support of earth, air, sun, moon, tides, plants, animals, society, strangers, family, friends, and all other things—the natural response is gratitude and humility.

These I express through thankfulness to Amida, my higher power who embodies all these things, and through acts of compassion and service toward my fellow beings and the planet.

Just Trusting

SSA IS RIGHTFULLY CONSIDERED one of Japan's greatest haiku masters. Himself a follower of Shinran, Issa's poems often express the deepest emotions of the nembutsu way. For instance, here is one of his haiku:

> the old wall's grass
> trusting...
> beads of dew

This is such a simple, small moment, yet it offers deep insight into the Shin approach to life. In the shade of an old wall, some grass clings humbly. It is nourished by the dew's moisture. The key to the poem, and to the life of shinjin that the poem subtly hints at, is in that single word of the second line: *trusting*.

Just as the grass lives on trust in the life-giving properties of the dew, so we are given true and real life in the trusting of power beyond the self. This trust finds expression in both the cosmic and mundane aspects of our experiences. For instance, my family and I moved from Los Angeles to Canada recently so that I could take a new job as a professor. Such life-changes certainly require lots of trust: trust that we would find new friends, trust that we would be able to live comfortably in a foreign country, trust that our love for one another would help us through the difficulties of such a big transition. And trust that wherever we go, we take the nembutsu with us.

This was the second time we'd moved away from a temple community. First it was a move to North Carolina—a state with no Jodo Shinshu representation—after several years of membership at the New York Buddhist Church. Then it was a move to a Canadian town without a Shin temple after two lovely years at West Los Angeles Buddhist Temple and the opportunity to visit many of the other temples of the Southern District. Each time we'd been sad to leave, and frankly it isn't fun being without regular access to a local sangha. But living away from temples, whether in the South or in Canada, has shown me that ultimately it is your own individual relationship with the Vow that is most essential. Community is a vital expression of the Buddha-way and a wonderful part of the Buddhist experience, but ultimately we have to say goodbye to even the most supportive sangha. Only the embrace of Other Power remains with us always and nurtures us even through the process of death.

Whatever old walls' shadows we may live in, we can all rely together on the Buddha's compassionate vow. Namu Amida Butsu.

Literal and Metaphorical

R EVEREND KENRYU TSUJI was a famous Jodo Shinshu minister who played an important role in both American and Canadian Shin Buddhism in the twentieth century. People who knew him still relate many amusing and compassionate stories about him. I remember one that I heard at a Buddhist temple in Richmond, Virginia, that he had founded. Richmond is a college town, and the temple attracted a good number of professors and students as members. Two fellows in particular were regular attendees and good friends, though with different approaches to Buddhism. One was a Chinese-American professor who had a Buddhist background, and the other was a European-American professor who had converted to Buddhism. Both practiced Pure Land Buddhism with Reverend Tsuji, and like most people they had their own hang-ups and issues—which led them to pester the minister with different questions.

The Chinese-American professor was a devout Buddhist with a somewhat conservative frame of mind toward Buddhism. His friend was a more philosophical Buddhist, inclined to question things and sometimes unable to commit himself sufficiently. Both of them often asked Reverend Tsuji to clarify the nature of Amida Buddha so that they could put their minds at rest. Secretly, as one of them told me later, they each hoped Reverend Tsuji would confirm a view that conformed to their own biases.

One day, after the weekly service, the Chinese-American professor approached Reverend Tsuji and asked, "Amida Buddha—is he real or a myth?" Reverend Tsuji smiled and said, "Amida is a metaphor." The professor went away in thought. The other man jumped up, pleased to hear a teaching that seemed to cement his personal prejudices. He walked over to Reverend Tsuji and said, "So, it's true, Amida doesn't literally exist, he's just a metaphor." Without a moment of hesitation, Reverend Tsuji told him, "Oh no, Amida is very real."

Each man got a teaching that shook up his fossilized views, forcing him to consider other ways of approaching the tradition, and thus notice the way even notions of Amida are used to reinforce our egoistic desires.

This kind of skillful means is an expression of the compassion valued by Shin Buddhism, which both meets you where you are, and, when you are ready, challenges you to go further.

Vegas Memorial

A LAS VEGAS CASINO hotel room with a party-size in-room tub isn't really the ideal place to hold a Buddhist memorial service.

But that's where my wife and I found ourselves when the one-year anniversary of my grandmother's death arrived, and even in the most crass corners of samsara we need to remember the things we truly value. I scrounged through our possessions in order to erect a makeshift altar: a bag of M&Ms and a cup of ice water (the cup had held a $1 margarita the night before), a photo of my grandmother, and an inch-high ceramic Buddha I'd picked up in a knick-knack shop. With the ringing of slot machines and crooning of celebrity impersonators filtering in from elsewhere in the hotel, my wife and I bowed our heads and reflected on how Grandmother touched our lives.

We came to live with and care for my grandmother in North Carolina at the beginning of 2001, leaving behind jobs and friends (and crime, pollution, and overcrowding) in New York City. At age ninety-five she was still living on her own, fiercely determined to be independent despite being legally blind, diabetic, and too weak to climb stairs without assistance. Her situation wasn't good: she'd recently had major surgery to remove a large tumor in her colon. The doctors weren't sure she'd survive the operation, and they told her she'd need at least four weeks of in-patient recovery when it was over. But she went under the knife and six days later was home sitting at the head of the Thanksgiving dinner table, surrounded by family. Among those who knew my grandmother, her stamina and ability to bounce back were legendary. Over the years she'd fallen down stairs, cracked her head on furniture, and fought through cancer, strokes, heart trouble, and a bleeding gastritis that leaked out half her blood volume. One time in Texas she accidentally stepped on the gas instead of the brake, ran over my great aunt Eula Belle and me, and plowed into the wall of a restaurant. Another time, back in the Twenties, she shot an attacking alligator in the eye while her date cowered in the bottom of the boat. Grandmother was a survivor.

But no one wins the battle against age, illness, and mortality, and by the time my wife and I arrived it was clear that she needed more assistance. Living with Grandmother kept her out of nursing facilities, and with us and the help of others she was able to continue her reign as the family matriarch. Religion was a strong factor in my decision to move in with her—Buddhism emphasizes gratitude and service, and respect for one's elders. Ignorance, the bogeyman of Buddhism, formed a fair part of the decision as well: we were committed to doing what it took to make Grandmother happy, but there was no way of knowing ahead of time just how demanding such a commitment could be.

When you live with someone in his or her mid-nineties, you

gradually come to understand that the traditional Buddhist formulation of old age, illness, and death as the three basic facts of suffering is dead-on. You can gain tremendous success in life, raise a big family, have an exciting job, develop a rich spiritual life, spend your time helping others—life offers lots of opportunities for the time we're here. But no matter how much you achieve, aging, sickness, and mortality are working away, whittling you down to size until the day they finally win for good. Like circling sharks, or baying hounds, they harry even the happiest of lives.

Over time, as I watched Grandmother's health rise and fall, I came to realize that old age, illness, and death are not actually three separate, isolated phenomena, but rather are completely intermeshed. To be old is to be frequently sick and to have death ever nearby as a possibility. To be sick is to be aware of one's aging and mortality. And death lies always at the end of the road—when we remember it we fear aging and illness, which hasten the inevitable. Buddhism is insightful to call attention to these three, yet the dogmatic approach can tend to obscure their interrelatedness.

Perhaps the tendency to harden insight into unquestioned doctrine arises from our need to feel secure, to gain a hold on our situation and stave off the fear that things are dangerous and beyond our control. It's an attitude that naturally appears when dealing with illness, aging, and mortality—the greatest of fears—and the fact that we really aren't in control, that we can't wield power over such awesome eventualities, just makes us crave answers and solutions all the more.

In a similar way, the modern formulation of the stages of grief popularized by Elisabeth Kübler-Ross offers a guidepost on the way of loss for the bereft, yet if taken literally, it denies how we revolve continuously in these mental states. Contrary to the most common understanding of this process, denial, anger, bargaining, depression, and acceptance are not discrete states arriving in a pre-determined order, with one stage being entered and another being left behind once and for all.

Since Grandmother's death, I may experience all of them in seemingly random order during the course of a day. At the grocery store I consider whether to buy tomatoes and make Grandmother some hoppin' john (a Southern concoction with okra and black-eyed peas), even though she's not waiting at home anymore. Later, I'm sad that I can't hear her stories anymore and that she'll just be another old dead person to my son. Later still I feel I've accepted her passing, only to catch myself daydreaming about how I might've done something to prevent the stroke that finally got her. You don't pass through each stage of grief, never to return. Instead, they all become your new companions, your inadequate replacements for the person you've lost for good. Your mind becomes a house haunted by the ghost of your loved one.

One Buddhist concept that sheds light on this process for me is that of *ichinen sanzen* (literally, "one thought three thousand") the mutual possession of and interpenetration of the three thousand mental worlds within the space of a single thought, formulated by the Chinese monk Tiantai. All of the possible mental states, from enlightenment to utter ignorance and depravity, exist as potentials within us at every moment. With our thoughts, speech, and actions we can call forth and embody any of them, and we may backslide into any from the force of karma or habit. The interconnectedness of all things means that both happiness and depression lie just a moment away, waiting for the right trigger to manifest in our lives. And so it goes: there is joy in my grief, anger in my gratitude, fear and desperation in my attempts to humbly accept the world. The grieving process spans three thousand mental worlds and then some, with room left over for dreams and fantasies.

In the midst of my grief, Reverend Taitetsu Unno told me one afternoon at the American Buddhist Studies Center that "death ends a life but not a relationship." This is a quote from *Tuesdays With Morrie* by Mitch Albom. Eventually I realized that this is really true—I still mold my life to fit Grandmother's whims and steer according to her example, even though she isn't around anymore to offer her judgments and encouragement.

Struggling with teaching and so many commitments, I have to pause and consider whether you can really make a dead person proud. On the other hand, is it really possible possible to let a dead person down? In Shin Buddhism we say that when someone dies they immediately go to the Pure Land, the realm of true reality, and then return to help those still trapped in the world of suffering. In a way, this expresses my feelings. My grandmother is gone, but still present. Her suffering is ended, but her support and lessons continue.

One lesson I learned, and learned hard, is that death really is suffering. At the very end, Grandmother languished for three and a half weeks, with bedsores, paralysis, and pain. It was a relatively good death—at home, with family, under medical care, and in bed, after an amazingly long and colorful life. But still it was difficult. Let's not fool ourselves: waiting at the end of our current adventures is almost certainly the worst experience we'll ever have.

Spirituality can sometimes prepare us to face this experience, but also often papers over it, sugarcoating the finality of our extinction until the actual moment arrives, and all the wrapping-paper falls away to reveal the stark truth. Old age, illness, and death aren't words in some old Indian book—they are the real facts of human existence, more real and enduring than anything we do or create during our short individual lives.

This was all driven home for me one night several months before Grandmother died. Sound asleep, I was awakened by the clanging of the old dinner bell she kept by her bed to summon me in emergencies. I went downstairs and found her sick, doubled-over on the bed. "I'm feeling bad. Stay with me," she pleaded. As the night passed, she would retch and vomit up black blood, then fall into a fitful sleep from the exhaustion of her ordeal until she woke to throw up again. I gave her medicine, changed her soiled clothes and bed-sheets, cleaned the floor, helped her off and on the toilet again and again.

Somewhere in the middle of the night I began to do *tonglen,* a Tibetan Buddhist practice that involves visualizing a person's pain as a black cloud, breathing it into oneself, and returning it on the out-breath as a healing, soothing white cloud. The tonglen helped me to stay with Grandmother and do my best, but really there was nothing I could do to take her pain away. It was a fact of age and illness, unassailable by my efforts or desires. Likewise, when it was time for her to die, there was nothing to do but let it happen.

As real and final as death is, I learned another lesson from Grandmother when she passed away. It sounds corny to those who aren't dealing with the aftershocks of death, but the truth is, life does in fact go on. It becomes a series of moments, slowly unfolding one after another as you deal with each day in turn.

Following the Buddhist traditions, I found a roadmap that gave me things to do as I worked to find meaning in my post-Grandmother life. I performed the appropriate Buddhist actions: I had a memorial service carried out at my temple, built a birdhouse to make merit (taken not literally in Jodo Shinshu, but as a form of symbolic thanksgiving), and placed a picture of Grandmother on my altar. These actions aren't understood as directed toward the deceased—the dead person has either gone to the Pure Land, or, if you're of a more figurative (or cynical) mindset, has disappeared and is gone. Either way, it's not the dead who need help or comfort, but the survivors. The dead have the easy job—they just have to stay dead. But those who continue after them have to find paths back to stability and happiness. And so religion appears again to offer wisdom, both pre-fabricated and hard-won, to fit the situation.

A famous Buddhist story tells of Kisa Gotami, a young mother from the Buddha's clan whose baby boy died suddenly. Grief-stricken, she carried his corpse with her everywhere, wailing and wondering aloud why her child had left her. People pitied her, and eventually she was told to go to the Buddha for advice. When she reached his retreat, she begged that the Buddha bring her boy back to life. Somewhat surprisingly, the Buddha agreed to do so—but first asked Gotami to do something. "Anything, anything," she cried in desperate hope. The Buddha told her to go into the village and bring back a mustard seed from a house that had never known death.

Kisa Gotami went from house to house, still clutching the limp body of her child, asking for mustard seeds. People readily agreed to give her one, but when she asked if anyone had died in the house, every time the occupants nodded sadly. In each house there had been some sort of loss—a father, a sister, an aunt, a baby. As Gotami made her way through the village, she gradually began to understand that death was an absolute and universal fact of existence, that no one escaped it, not in the meanest hut or in the palace itself. Finally, she took her child's body to the charnel ground and left it, returning to the Buddha to be ordained as a nun. Realizing that the Buddha never meant to resurrect her boy but was teaching her a more important religious lesson, she released her attachment and, with newfound wisdom, committed herself to a life of spiritual awakening.

I've read or been told this story dozens of times. Before, I always marveled at the truth of this tale, its brave acceptance of the way of things, and the Buddha's humble demonstration of a spiritual fact more important than the healing of flesh. And I've told this story more times that I can recall, confident in its correctness and value.

But then Grandmother died—and without my knowing it, the story completely changed. The first time I read about Kisa Gotami again after Grandmother's death, I immediately thought, "If Buddha had played a trick like that on me, I would've torn his goddamn head off!"

The truth is, I'd much rather have Grandmother back than to acquire some piece of spiritual insight. I'd eagerly trade in all my books and statues, my altar, and all the teachings I've attended and blessings I've received. If Jesus had been around handing out resurrections, I would've surely picked him over the do-nothing-because-it's-a-learning-experience Buddha.

Hard-won religious understanding is a very poor substitute for the love and support of someone close to you. But whether or not it takes second place, it's all you end up with. Everyone is going to die on you, until the day that you die on whomever is left. So learning from the worst, immutable parts of life, or just continuing to revolve in painful ignorance, is the only choice we get. Buddha's story may have a disappointing punchline, but that doesn't mean he wasn't right.

In that Vegas hotel room, my wife and I finished our sutra-chanting, and I prepared to read aloud an epistle by Rennyo, the charismatic

Shin leader who helped spread the Pure Land teachings throughout medieval Japan. His brief letter reveals an intimate knowledge
of how old age, illness, and death await us all, an understanding
born from the deaths of four wives and seven children over the
course of an eighty-five-year-long lifetime. Yet while Rennyo feels
genuine grief, ultimately these losses become the occasion for awakening wisdom and compassion:

> Though loved ones gather and lament, everything is to no
> avail. The body is then sent into an open field and vanishes
> from this world with the smoke of cremation, leaving only
> white ashes. There is nothing more real than this truth of life.
> The fragile nature of human existence underlies both the
> young and the old, and therefore we must, one and all, turn
> to the teachings of the Buddha and awaken to the ultimate
> source of life.
>
> By so understanding the meaning of death, we shall come
> to fully appreciate the meaning of this life which is unrepeat-
> able and thus to be treasured above all else. By virtue of true
> compassion, let us realize the irreplaceable value of human
> life and let us together live the nembutsu in our lives.

The nembutsu is the central activity of Shin Buddhism, an
expression of joy that arises when one realizes that one is embraced
and supported by the infinite compassion of all things. Learning to
live a life of gratitude is what this practice is about. I thought Rennyo's sentiments were echoed by a quote from Antoine de Saint-
Exupery that was read at Grandmother's funeral: "We live not by
things, but by the meanings of things." If this is true, then it isn't the
cold fact of Grandmother's life and death that ultimately matter, but
what I take from them.

In an era that so often hides death and suffering, when our elders are squirreled away in nursing homes and corpses are painted to appear lifelike at their funerals, I know I'll never think about aging, sickness, and death in the same way again. Grandmother's struggle and loss, the pain of old age and the continuing potential for happiness that persists until the very final moment, are truths as solid as anything the Buddha taught. These truths call me to remembrance, whether I'm seated in my home temple or a glitzy casino. When you finally touch reality on this level, there is nothing left to do but to say "Thank you, thank you."

Thank you for joy and sorrow, for death and new life, for caregivers and the opportunity to help.

Thank you for love while it lasts, for memories that endure.

And thank you for grandmothers.

Meat and Eating Disorders

RECENTLY, I encountered a Buddhist in a difficult situation. After struggling with eating disorders such as anorexia, she was ready to get professional treatment. But the facilities that were available to her all insisted that she eat meat—there was a clause that she must agree to eat at least one chicken and one fish, in part because faked vegetarianism is apparently used as an excuse by anorexics not to eat. As a committed vegetarian who felt that her understanding of Buddhism necessitated a non-carnivorous lifestyle, she was in a real dilemma. She wanted and needed the treatment, but was extremely disturbed that it would require her to eat meat.

Thankfully, I have never needed treatment for serious eating disorders. In offering her advice, I had to imagine how I might act in her situation, which had no perfect answer. I have been a vegetarian for about a dozen years. It is not required in Shin Buddhism, and my reading of the historical record is that the Buddha was not a vegetarian and did not require it of his followers. Shinran wasn't a vegetarian, and his ability to interact with the peasants and fisher-men on their level was part of what made his Buddhism so com-pelling to them. However, concern for non-human beings is a strong current within all forms of Buddhism, and vegetarianism has been a significant minority position, especially in East Asia. Person-ally, I support a vegetarian approach to Buddhism for those who are able to do so.

In my friend's situation, I counseled her to eat the meat. We need to understand that part of practicing compassion and wisdom means being willing to take the help that is available to us. When you have a serious illness, your family, friends, and community want you to get better, and you're not helping anyone (yourself included) by avoiding treatment that you need.

In Buddhism, among the virtues we seek to cultivate is flexibil-ity, best expressed in the concept of skillful means. Situations differ, and we have to meet them with our life, not dogmas or precon-ceived notions. Usually, it is perhaps best not to eat meat. But, there are cases where eating meat for a short time may be the lesser of the various "evils" available to you.

The chicken and the fish she will meet at the clinic are bodhi-sattvas who have given their lives to her in order that she may break the unhealthy attachments she possesses to food/body issues, men-tal unclarity, and trauma. Before she even signed up for the program that chicken and that fish were already fulfillfing their karma in this way, for her or for some other person in need. Consuming their offered bodies in mindful reverence is not the same thing as contin-uing in a lifestyle of meat-eating, which extracts countless beings from the world for our nourishment and pleasure that otherwise might not have been killed.

If it were me, as much as the idea makes me queasy, as wrong as I feel it is to kill and consume other beings, I would eat the chicken and fish. First, I would bow my head and think about how they have become bodhisattvas for me and how grateful I feel toward them. Next, I would bring to mind all the causes and conditions that go into this meal and all meals which I receive, how my nourishment always makes a negative impact on the lives of others in ways I cannot perceive, and also how my nourishment makes a positive impact on others too. Then, I would eat the chicken and fish in a spirit of thanksgiving.

I would try to enjoy the meal in order to show the most respect to those brother beings who made this sacrifice. Afterward, I would say "Namu Amida Butsu" to thank them and all who support my life. Then, I would redouble my commitment not to eat meat in the future when I am out of the program. Whenever I felt tempted to eat meat or in some other way contribute to the suffering of animal beings, I would recall the sacrifice of these two bodhisattvas and remember that they would not wish me to commit wrong actions. And perhaps, if I were in a future situation where I could do so, I would repay this kindness by making a donation or volunteering for a vegetarian-awareness organization, PETA, or some other animal-friendly organization like a dog shelter.

This is only how I, as one fully vegetarian Buddhist, would handle the situation. I feel for all those caught between their desire to fulfill the precepts and their need to break life-threatening attachments.

False Impression

ONE TIME, after a lecture, two students approached Tai Unno and asked him, "Mister Unno, are you enlightened?" He shook his head. "No, I intend to take one hundred lifetimes to reach enlightenment."

The students went away, excitedly whispering, "Wow, he really is enlightened!"

It's so easy to see what we want in other people.

Rebirth vs. No-Self

MANY SHIN TEMPLES hold study classes, and I always enjoyed the Thursday gathering at the West Los Angeles Buddhist Temple when time allowed me to attend. People come prepared to air their most knotty confusion in the hopes that Reverend Fumiaki Usuki and the others will be able to clarify matters. Sometimes we do manage to answer such questions; often we don't. But either way I really admire how nothing is off-limits in Reverend Usuki's study class and he doesn't pretend to always have every answer. I think this kind of openness and honesty is very important in Buddhism.

I recall one question that struck right at the heart of Buddhist thought: if there is "no self," then what does rebirth mean? How can you be reborn if there's no "you" to begin with?

This is a paradox that all schools of Buddhism have struggled with. In fact, because there are many forms of Buddhism, this question has been answered in many different ways. I want to provide my own approach to the subject. I don't pretend it is the "right" one—it is just another attempt by yet another Buddhist to deal with this issue.

As I understand it, there is a crucial core to Buddhist thought, and then there are many other beliefs and attitudes that act as support or ways of teaching that are not as fundamentally important. Sometimes these two things conflict with each other. If you are unable to resolve these conflicts, you should hold to what is central and discard or at least leave alone what is less important. This was the method of Shinran and his teacher Honen, for instance.

Beliefs about previous lives, giant talking snakes *(nagas),* the great Mount Sumeru at the center of the world, and other things were common in India before and during the Buddha's lifetime, and there is nothing particularly Buddhist about them. They are just part of the shared religious atmosphere of India. But the Buddha did pronounce four marks of existence that are utterly unique to Buddhism and that he considered to be the most important aspects of his Dharma. These unique Buddhist contributions to human religion are (1) there is a degree of suffering in all unawakened human experiences, (2) there is no unchanging self or soul, (3) there is nothing truly permanent anywhere in the universe, and (4) there is peace and liberation obtainable through awakening (known as "nirvana" or, in the case of Shin, "the Pure Land" or "the Realm of Bliss"). All forms of Buddhism, no matter what else they disagree on, hold true to these four teachings.

When we talk about no-self, it means that there isn't some sort of eternal spirit hiding somewhere deep inside the body or mind and that constitutes our "true" identity. Instead, we exist as collections of different parts (bones, brains, blood, etc.), mental states (thoughtful, sleepy, hungry, etc.), and relationships (son, father, brother, husband, etc.). These parts are changing all the time, and as they change, we change. We never stay the same, even from one moment to the next. But we tend to cling to ideas about ourselves (and others) and are slow to change, and so we suffer. This is certainly true in my own life.

And, while all schools of Buddhism agree whole-heartedly on no-self, they disagree about rebirth: there are many rather different interpretations of this idea. Many Tibetans talk about a subtle level of the consciousness as being "reincarnated," for example, while many Thai talk about karma as what is reborn. Because there is no agreement, I find the thing most helpful to me is to put this question aside as secondary.

There is a famous recorded dialogue of the Buddha, where someone asked him if anything survives after death, and the Buddha said that this is not an important question: what is important, he said, was to understand the way of freedom from suffering.

Some scholars say that no-self and previous lives don't really fit together, and that the Buddha probably only talked about this because his Indian audience couldn't understand religion if he left it completely out. That may be true, but I don't think we can ever be sure either way. And indeed, all forms of Buddhism that have survived until today do carry beliefs about rebirth, if not reincarnation, in one way or another.

For me, the question of "previous lives" or future reincarnation is not an important issue. I may have lived many lifetimes before this one, but I don't have any way of knowing for sure. What I do understand is that I am embraced by Amida, so I don't have to worry about anything bad happening to me after I die. That means future reincarnation isn't an issue for me either. With the past and the future taken care of as issues for me, I am enabled to focus on this present lifetime and apply the Dharma to what I can see and understand: the here and now. In the here and now, there is no permanent "Jeff" that never changes.

Instead, this Jeff is always dying (changing from what I was) and being reborn (becoming something new) moment to moment. In the present life, no-self and rebirth are completely intertwined. It is because there is no self that I am reborn every day. If there were some fossilized, permanent Jeff-self, then I would never change and never be able to adapt to life as it comes. If there were no rebirth, I'd be stuck forever as a baby or a surly teenager or a guy who hadn't learned about Buddhism yet. So when I reflect on these things in this way, no-self and rebirth stop being confusing ideas about metaphysics and the afterlife, and instead become sources of gratitude for me.

I don't claim I've settled the issue of no-self vs. reincarnation or rebirth here. Ultimately, each person has to come to a balanced understanding of her or his own. But in sharing a little of how I, as one Shin follower, have approached these issues, I hope I can point out how others might also fruitfully deal with them. I am not sad that I have no permanent soul, that everything changes, and that I'm always being recreated day by day. It is these facts that offer me some hope of living the way of nembutsu.

Often I am overwhelmed by all the stress and responsibility in my life. But I am never *permanently* stressed or overwhelmed. Just as often, a sudden moment comes when I wake up to all the forces that are supporting me in every situation, and I am reborn as a thankful person who can't help saying "Namu Amida Butsu!" And then I am grateful that I am able to change from my self-obsession toward a more Buddhist attitude.

In this way, I guess rebirth is important to me after all. Whenever we turn away from self-centeredness we are born once again in the Pure Land.

All-Embracing

A T ONE TIME, an illiterate myokonin named Shoma who did manual labor for a living was staying at a Jodo Shinshu temple. The priest had been reading one of the Pure Land Sutras and had a thought, which he expressed out loud: "What is the meaning of the phrase 'Amida's compassion embraces all beings, forsaking none?'"

Shoma jumped up, flung his arms wide, and began speaking in a loud voice. The priest thought Shoma had gone crazy and went running away. Shoma raced after him, close behind. They ran back and forth in the worship hall, the priest's robes flapping like a giant black crow trying to raise itself into the air. Finally the priest ducked down a corridor and hid himself in a closet.

Shoma came pounding down the hallway and stopped outside the closet. "Priest, I am here!" he shouted. Then he threw the closet door open and stood there with his arms outstretched. In a booming voice he said, "This is the meaning of the phrase, 'embracing all beings, forsaking none!'"

The priest laughed and said joyfully, "Now I understand. That which never lets me go, despite all my desperate attempts to escape or deny it—that is the meaning of embracing all beings and forsaking none."

I always loved this story—I can just picture the terrified priest running wide-eyed away from the hulking Shoma, who chases after him determined to viscerally show how Amida never, ever stops working to bring all beings to awakening. This active nature is a hallmark of Amida in the Shin school of Buddhism.

For instance, Shin statues of Amida typically are standing, not sitting in quiet meditation, as if they are ready to spring into action. Furthermore, they lean ever so slightly forward toward the viewer, indicating that Amida actually comes to rescue suffering beings by working in their lives, rather than waiting passively in the Pure Land for beings that are able to qualify to come to him. In Jodo Shinshu, everyone qualifies for the Pure Land *exactly by virtue of being unawakened*—the only ticket you need for admittance is to not be a Buddha, and therefore to be a proper object of infinite, never-ending compassion.

There is a Buddha statue in Kyoto that I have always felt best expresses this ideal. It is housed in Eikando, a famous Jodo Shu temple. Eikando is a beautiful temple, with graceful stairways and halls. If you climb high enough into the grounds, you find a chapel dedicated to Amida. The statue inside is rather unique: the Buddha is standing and looking backward over his left shoulder, rather than directly facing the viewer. This is the Amida-Who-Looks-Back. To me it wonderfully sums up the intentions of the Pure Land school. For people who aren't able to understand the abstruse doctrines of the sutras (or, in previous times, weren't able to read at all), this statue has been provided to directly show everyone what Amida's compassion is like. Amida is proceeding toward the Pure Land, but the buddha's mind is solely on the beings who need further help to be liberated. Amida looks back continually, checking to see that we are keeping up and ready to go back again and again to the suffering world until everyone, with no exceptions, is released from pain and awakened to deepest reality. This is a concrete representation of the Sutra teaching that Amida embraces *everyone,* forsaking *none,* no matter who they are or what they are like, no matter if they are Buddhist or not, regardless of their good acts or evil deeds. As long as space endures and ever after if need be, Amida works tirelessly to help others, no strings attached.

And though we may not be able to fully follow this example ourselves, it provides a role model for how we should act toward our fellow beings, with non-discriminating love and compassion.

Off the Wagon

USED TO BE an absolute, unyielding teetotaler. I never had anything to drink until I was twenty-three—whereas in my home-
town many people started as early as middle school. I have still
never smoked a cigarette or taken any drugs classified as illegal by
the US government. I was also a vegan for six years, a type of vegetarian who will not even eat dairy or eggs.

My rigid stance on intoxicants came long before my explicit
interest in and later commitment to Buddhism. I just always felt that
these substances did enormous harm to the individual and society,
and basically viewed them as literally evil. When I became a Buddhist, I interpreted the fifth precept as supporting my views: it says
that Buddhists should avoid intoxicants. Abstinence is of course a
good idea in many cases, since on the one hand it prevents losing
control and causing harm to others, and on the other hand alcohol
clouds the mind, essentially preventing the awareness that Buddhism promotes.

Now much of my attitude has changed. I drink pretty frequently with friends and family, and have gone back to eating dairy and eggs, though not meat. And I am much happier.

The change occurred when I realized that I was using my natural self-restraint to nurse my ego, secretly building up ideas like "Jeff doesn't drink; he's more moral and self-controlled than others" and "Jeff must therefore be a better Buddhist." I felt encouraged in these rather un-spiritual thoughts by my Zen studies when I was younger, since much of Zen is about self-power, about you yourself sitting and wrestling with koans and having a great breakthrough and becoming enlightened. Of course, in some ways this just shows that I was a poor Zen student. I figured not drinking put me one step closer to enlightenment than those slobs who partook of a beer or two on the weekend with their friends. In other words: I was becoming an insufferable jerk. Even worse, I was convincing myself I was actually being *holy* with my arrogance and attachment to precepts.

But now, as I've said, I feel differently. Before, I had an exterior holiness, a veneer, but inside I was just as blindly passionate and egotistical as other people; actually, I was probably even more so. So, I had to switch and become just what I was. Now I drink sometimes, and enjoy it (a big surprise to me!), and don't worry because I'm not such a hypocrite anymore. I'd rather just wear my faults on my sleeve and try to get back to really uncovering wisdom and compassion, instead of trying to get enlightened by being a snob.

Now my perspective on the fifth precept is that if you're going to break it, then break it. Try to do it mindfully: don't drink too much, don't put yourself or others in dangerous situations (like driving afterward), and if possible, pay attention to how your mind is changing and maybe even learn something from it. But don't kid yourself, you're a human being, not a buddha, and you're going to feel the need to unwind sometimes. If you're not going to drink, make sure it's for the right reasons, and don't get egotistical about it.

Ego is a much larger impediment to awakening than a couple Budweisers every now and then.

Relationships Are the Realm
of Awakening

I USED TO THINK that awakening was achieved through actively controlling the mind, and I thought that there were two categories to my life: "Buddhist stuff" (meditating, studying Dharma, talking with teachers, etc.), which was good and useful, and "non-Buddhist stuff" (hanging out with friends, visiting my family, watching TV, eating ice cream, lying on the couch doing nothing, letting my mind wander, etc.), which was unproductive and in some nebulous way all contributed to my suffering-laden attachment to "worldly" things. I tried very hard to be a "perfect Buddhist," letting friendships slip in favor of quiet time for self-reflection, distancing myself somewhat from family, disdaining secular culture and activities as distractions.

But eventually I discovered that I wasn't up to snuff. There was just no way I was going to be able to cut myself off from the world, both because I'm hopelessly entangled, and because part of me fundamentally doesn't *want* to live on a mountaintop forever. I was just no sage, no matter how hard I wanted to be one.

Letting go of attachment to "Buddhist" things was very difficult. I wondered if I'd wasted my time pursuing an impossible goal. Or conversely, was I about to waste all the time and effort I'd put into my quest for enlightenment by returning to a normal pattern of life? Was I succumbing to my delusional passions? If I couldn't clearly demarcate the "good" from the "bad" in my life, the "religious" from the "worldly," how could I chart a path to true peace of mind?

Nonetheless, I did manage to let go of some of my religious attachments. But luckily, I also learned a lot of lessons by giving up my idea that I was somehow treading the good and narrow path. First of all, I think an awakening that can't cope with the real world is probably half-baked at best. The Dharmakaya, the ultimate interconnectedness of all things, the perception of which is equated with enlightenment in the Mahayana view, includes the sacred and the profane, the monastery and all the sitcoms, college-buddies, ex-girlfriends, casual acquaintances, traffic jams, and rainy days put together. After all, how could a true awakening not include 99% of life? Also, in Buddhism we believe that true wisdom is compassion; perfect compassion is the fulfillment of perfect wisdom. Where are we to be compassionate, if not right here and now in our relationships to other people?

Before, I thought of relationships as fetters that held me back from the hard work needed to achieve insight. But now my attitude is completely different. I don't think my relationships are ropes tying me down; I don't even think that I can experience awakening "regardless" of them. Rather, I've come to believe that these relationships are the single greatest learning opportunities we could hope for, and furthermore, that it is movement toward peace, ease, compassion, and wisdom within these entanglements that signifies true Buddhist awakening and attainment.

Buddhism is about coming to know the self—not the little,

ego-bound "me, myself, and I" self, but the big self, the true self, which includes everything in perfect interpenetration, utterly without hindrance anywhere. For me, these human relationships are an important part of that self, the self beyond my skin-barrier, which includes all my friendships, relations, business transactions, environmental impact, consumption of food, services created through other people's labor, and so on. Dozens of complete strangers and I exchange carbon dioxide on the subway each morning—they too are part of the whole that comprises me, just as I am a facet, however small, of the existence of everyone and everything that exists. And I feel that as I learn to recognize this vast, impersonal (and yet somehow intimate), karmically-driven network of relationships for what it is, and furthermore learn to operate compassionately toward all beings/things within this framework, with kindness and humility, then I come just about as close to enlightenment as a hopeless stubborn fool like me could ever be.

Meditation, chanting, reading sutras—these are all tools that can be useful under the right circumstances. But I think there's just as much (if not more) Buddhism in giving my wife a hug when she comes home from a long day, in dropping a buck in the homeless woman's cup on the corner, in waiting until everyone gets off the train before trying to push my way inside. And in seeing the Buddha within everyone, and recognizing these relationships, major and minor, as aspects of the Dharmakaya, marked by shunyata and thus no hindrance, just part of the ebb and flow of emptiness's form.

In a way, I find it very easy to chant sutras and pat myself on the back for being a "good" Buddhist—which is why I know there's no real attainment there. But I still struggle mightily not to curse the fat woman very slowly going up the stairs in front of me, or the telemarketers who keep bugging me every night—and so I know these are the real places for application of the Dharma, the stubborn knots in Indra's Net that I have to work with to smooth out. I can't learn that by shaving my head or renouncing my friends and family; I can only learn it by accepting my life and myself just as I am, and discovering how to let a Dharmic view transform my everyday thoughts and deeds.

Hearing and Listening

MONPO—HEARING THE DHARMA—is a key concept in Shin Buddhism. Where some Buddhisms employ a visual metaphor for awakening (seeing reality, observing one's true self, etc.), Shin tends to employ auditory ones. The difference is subtle but significant. Hearing is receptive, open: it implies that you receive something from another, rather than assertively seeing it yourself with penetrating eyesight. This is a manifestation of Shin Buddhism's emphasis on humility and receptiveness, the better to abandon reliance on the false ego-self.

Even though it may seem easy enough, hearing is actually rather difficult when you attempt to do it in an intentional way. For example, even in everyday conversation we may wish to listen to others, but often our mind wanders—either we get distracted, or bored, or, in many cases, we start composing our reply while our conversation partner is still talking. Likewise, when trying to listen to the Dharma—whether it comes to us at temple, while talking with friends and mentors, or while walking silently in nature—we are apt to lose our attention and get entangled in thoughts, especially self-oriented ones.

Returning to simple listening after being caught in distraction can be likened to how Buddhist meditators return to their breath after getting lost in thought. Like meditation, listening *deeply* takes practice. Yet it is not a strenuous sort of exercise. For a moment or a day, listening is something we all can do. And when we realize that we are no longer listening, we just smile, nod, and start listening again. Because there is no end goal other than to settle further into the Dharma, there is no need for self-recrimination if we lose the way for a while.

We just re-open ourselves to the Dharma and let it continue its work of freeing us from our foolishness.

Scattered Nenju

YOU CAN OFTEN spot a Buddhist when you're out in the world by the string of beads we sometimes wear on our left wrists. This is like a rosary in some ways, though it predates the use of such beads in the Catholic tradition. In Japanese these are most often called *juzu,* which means "counting beads." But Shin Buddhism has a special term for these: we usually call them *nenju.* This means "thinking beads." The reason is that we don't use rosaries to count the number of our recitations and try to gain merit thereby like other sects do—we use them as a reminder of Amida's compassion that has already been fulfilled.

Nenju are supposed to be treated respectfully. At the same time, they are part of the overall Shin attitude of being easygoing and flexible. So for instance during a service at the West Los Angeles Buddhist Temple one time, the nenju of one of the Dharma School kids broke while the children were all gathering for incense offering. Technically, the children should have maintained composure and gone through the offering without wavering. But instead they all started scrabbling about on the floor of the worship hall, chasing beads and giving them back to the kid who lost them. The minister thought this was correct and actually changed his sermon to talk about the incident. As he explained, when people first get involved in Jodo Shinshu they often are obsessed with getting the forms right, with following the letter of Shinran's teachings, and with following all the traditions.

But as we sink into the Vow, we gradually come to realize that in Shin Buddhism what matters is not formality but warmth, not the letter but the implicit meaning, not the traditions themselves but the mind of gratitude and open-heartedness that they are designed to provoke. So the minister thanked the children for showing with their spontaneity the true spirit of Shin Buddhism by helping their friend pick up his lost beads, even in the middle of a solemn ceremony while the adults were waiting on them.

Form and Content

Kogi Kudara, a professor at the Jodo Shinshu–affiliated Ryukoku University in Kyoto, wrote an interesting essay titled "My Impression Regarding Amida Belief." I thought the concluding paragraphs were especially insightful:

> Sometimes we hear some people speaking about Amida Buddha or the Pure Land as substantial existences, as if they are the same as God or heaven in Christianity. But that kind of explanation is beside the point. Amida Buddha is like a mirror that shows one's true self in order to fulfill the supreme self (the expression of the concept of compassion in the form of the personified Buddha). […] We have to understand that "forms without content are meaningless, and content without form is disorder." Living in the modern world, we should not lose the content and not be constricted by forms or formality.

I really liked this point about Amida as a mirror that shows our true selves. This is true for both aspects of Amida, the one with form and the formless one. As Buddha with form, Amida symbolizes the perfection of human awakening, something beyond our own capacities, and thus reveals to us our deeply ignorant state as deluded beings. But at the same time, Amida as formless true reality reveals our inner togetherness with all things, pure and liberated beyond the dualities and grasping nature of the ego.

Amida, Other Power, Pure Land—these are forms meant to convey content: the universal Buddhist truths of emptiness, interdependence, and the perfection of things just as they are. Yet we have to be careful to balance these two things, form and content. If we just become attached to forms, like thinking of Amida and the Pure Land as substantial existences apart from the wisdom they are meant to convey, we risk falling into one sort of trap. But if we discard the forms then we lose our chance to interact with the content of Buddhism on anything but an intellectual, formal level. That's another sort of trap.

At best, we can aspire to hold on to the forms that have made the Pure Land way such a beautiful tradition, while also holding on to the content that has enlivened those forms and made them meaningful by keeping them in accord with deep Buddhist insight.

Just Existing

L IVING IN CANADA THESE DAYS, we have to put up with a lot more snow than we did in Los Angeles (to say the least!)—but even though I often have to do a bit of shoveling, I don't mind it at all. I grew up in Connecticut so I have a fondness for snow in the wintertime.

There is something so wonderful about snow. It is soft, quiet, humble, and very beautiful when it blankets the ground outside. Walking outside after a fresh snow is always very moving to me. It reminds me of one of Issa's greatest haiku:

Just existing
I exist...
Snow drifting down

I imagine Issa walking with me after another heavy snowstorm, maybe in Kyoto or Ontario, with the familiar world transformed into a new landscape of soft round edges and muffling pure white snow. A few tardy flakes are still falling haphazardly from the clearing sky, and the air is fresh and clean. Issa points to the simple miracle of our existence, just bare existence itself, a wonder greater than any act of nature. Snow is just drifting down, just as it is, and we are just walking along in appreciation, just as we are. Things are right in their naturalness, with nothing needed for joy beyond a few snowflakes and gratitude for our lives and the chance to experience beauty.

Like many of Issa's poems, this one works on another level as well. The snow may be taken for a model of ourselves. Just as it simply drifts down, so too we drift through life, just existing in the same manner as a snowflake—our lives are short, beautiful, unique. And when the time comes, the sun of Other Power shining on us melts our icy ignorance and returns us to the purity of clear water, merging once more with the all-embracing ocean.

There is a story about a myokonin that seems connected to this. Osono was traveling to Kyoto so she could attend a service at the Honganji temple. She saw some children building a snowman. Osono went over and began bowing to the snowman, much to the surprise of her traveling companions. They asked her why she was showing such gratitude to the snowman. Osono replied, "This snowman reveals to me the form of my trusting heart, and therefore I'm grateful. When the rays of the sun shine on the snowman, it will melt. Just like my trusting heart, the rays of Amida's compassion shine upon and guide me. The more I listen, the more my trusting heart melts away, and nothing remains, everything disappears. For this I'm grateful to the snowman."

Whether it snows, rains, or is 100 degrees, each day we express the amazing fact of our existence. If we can learn to be like Issa or Osono, embracing that fact in wonder and appreciation, then how blessed our lives become. A universe of supporting causes goes into the creation of each flake of snow and each human being.

Walking between snow drifts, murmuring nembutsu in the chilly air, building a snowman, just existing together with all things, what a touching thing it is to be alive.

Namu Amida Butsu.

Changing and Sharing

I N PRE-MODERN TIMES, Shin was often spread via reference to miracles, visions, supernatural saviors, and the charisma of individual leaders. The correctness of Shinran's doctrine was emphasized through stories about his vision of Prince Shotoku, one of the founders of Japanese Buddhism, often worshipped as a bodhisattva. These paintings displayed brilliantly colored Amidas descending in swirling clouds to save devotees—and tales of blissful activities in the Pure Land and torments in the hells abounded. This is how other sects spread too—Zen, for instance, was not the meditative, artistic elite we often think of, but spread mainly through its promotion of funeral services designed to "transfer merit" to deceased loved ones. All of Japanese Buddhism—Shin included—was, in this way, somewhat *otherworldly*.

If the extraordinary was given much greater emphasis within Shin in former times, what has changed to alter this? I think it must be that as modernity has impacted Jodo Shinshu in both Japan and overseas, new thinkers have sought ways to make Buddhism relevant to changed times. One of these methods has been to highlight the ever-present, but not always foregrounded, emphasis on the ordinary foolish person struggling with religion amid the toil of everyday life. We can see this in Zen too, which has been partially re-conceptualized from a highly ritualistic and hierarchical religion into a more individualized, meditative path, with a special attention given to the value of the quotidian.

So the shift toward greater emphasis on the ordinary within Shin and Zen has historical factors behind it. That doesn't mean that either former or current approaches are more correct, only that religion changes with the times. It may be that for some people, re-appropriating the extraordinary elements of Jodo Shinshu is a more attractive path. For others, the everyday will probably continue to command most of their attention. Since it all comes down to personal preferences, and since both styles have been used by Shin promoters and thinkers from the beginning, I think there must be room for a range of approaches to Jodo Shinshu in the modern world.

An issue that bothers some Shin traditionalists is that of taking elements of other paths to augment our own, for instance Zen meditation or vocabulary from other sects or sources. There's been some debate about this in Shin circles lately. I think we need to remember that all things are interdependent, Shin Buddhism included—they arise as nexuses of different component parts and are subject to constant change. The truth is, by Rennyo's time Shin Buddhism had already changed tremendously from what it was in Shinran's time, and naturally today Shin Buddhism is very different from either of those two earlier forms.

There is no pure core of Shin, nor any set of specifically Shin practices completely unrelated to other sects. Shin has always developed in conversation with the rest of Japanese religion and culture, and now in conversation with culture and religion in the

United States, Canada, and many other places. The things we think of as Shin elements—such as chants like Juseige, Junirai, and San-butsuge, oshoko (incense offering), nembutsu, etc.—all have their origins outside of Jodo Shinshu.

Furthermore, when we look at Shinran's magnum opus, *Kyo-gyoshinsho,* we find a book composed almost entirely of other texts, many of them outside of what we might consider the Pure Land tradition proper. Even *Shoshinge,* Shinran's moving account of his spiritual lineage, is essentially a list of teachers from non-Shin traditions. Shinran declared that his Pure Land forefathers were Nagarjuna the Madhyamikist, Vasubandhu the Yogacharin, Tan-luan the ex-Taoist, Tao-cho the Nirvana Sutra–devotee, Shan-tao the meditation master, Genshin the Tendai monk, and Honen the Jodo Shu founder.

Influences go both ways. Shin has been the largest sect in Japan for quite some time, and it has left its mark on many other schools. The married clergy one finds these days in Zen and Nichiren come from Shin precedents, for instance. For that matter, Nichiren's biggest influence was Honen, whose framework of single practice he lifted for his own use in promoting the primacy of chanting the title of the *Lotus Sutra.*

Jodo Shinshu has always taken elements from other schools of Buddhism and retrofitted them to a Shin sensibility. Today, for instance, when one attends services at the New York Buddhist Church, one chants the Three Refuges in Pali, sings hymns with organ accompaniment, and sits quietly in meditation for a few minutes before the chanting. I don't see this syncretic approach as threatening, and I believe that meditation, like other elements of general Buddhism, can be successfully "Shin-ized." In fact, meditation has been included in some Shin temples in Japan for at least a hundred years now.

However, people's cautions about these issues have to be taken very seriously. When exploring elements of other sects, we have to be careful to remember what we affirm as Shin Buddhists. If we perform meditation with the idea that it will *help us get into the Pure Land,* or take strict adherence to moral percepts as a *necessity* for awakening, we will muddy the waters of shinjin. But if someone meditates because it helps him as an individual calm down and remember the compassion of Amida, or if someone else endeavors to follow the precepts as an expression of gratitude for Amida's liberating Other Power, I don't see these actions as wrong in any way.

Each of us must weigh for ourselves how we wish to pursue our lives as Shin Buddhists, and what seems wrong to me may actually work well for you, while what is essential to you may have no particular relevance to my life. We do need to remain conscious about the possibility of transforming other practices into ego-solidifying self-efforts.

But that doesn't automatically preclude Shin Buddhists from finding responsible ways to integrate them into their overall Dharma paths.

What Have You Done Now?

PEOPLE WHO have been fortunate enough to learn from Tai Unno know that his wife, Alice, plays a big part in his teachings.

Alice is an ordained Shin priest in her own right, but she typically has expressed her ministry through nurturing mentally handicapped children. She is a warm, thoughtful person, and she often has something useful to add to whatever Dr. Unno talks about. At the same time, the amusing stories of their lives together and occasional squabbles make for good Dharma material in his sermons.

I remember one story Dr. Unno told about when he and Alice were living in Los Angeles. Puffed up at his own importance, he told Alice that she should take the garbage out since it wasn't a man's job (this was many decades ago, as you might be able to tell). Later that day, while talking to someone, he realized he was acting improperly and basically transferring his metaphorical garbage onto Alice—hardly fair of him to do. This insight puffed him up further as he marveled at his own wisdom and compassion. So he returned home triumphantly, certain that Alice would be impressed at his breakthrough. Walking in the door, he announced, "I will take out the garbage!" He looked at Alice expectantly, waiting for the beaming adoration and gratitude that he was sure she'd show.

Alice immediately narrowed her eyes in suspicion, searching his face for signs of guilt, and said, "All right, what have you done now?"

Green Rice

WHENEVER I READ the poetry of Issa, it seems that he has two meanings. One is the simple beautiful surface meaning, where he delights in the things of this world just as they are, giving thanks for being enabled to live a life in this bittersweet human world. But he often seems to have a deeper meaning too, where he points to the truths that his Jodo Shinshu religious training revealed to him. For instance, take this haiku of his:

Even poorly planted rice
slowly, slowly
becomes green!

On one level, this is a poem that extols the way rice seedlings struggle to manifest the life force within them, and eventually fulfill their potential by becoming green rice that basks in the sun and waves in the wind. Even when poorly planted by the farmers, they manage to persevere and become rice, achieving their destiny.

But there is another possible reading of this haiku as well.

We are the poorly planted rice, with our scant roots of good karma and many obstacles blocking our way to enlightenment. Like a poorly planted rice seedling, the odds are against us. Yet there is a life force stirring within each of us that yearns for the sun of awakening, and with the ever-present help of Other Power, we are slowly, slowly made to ripen into Buddhas. It may take a long time, but we are promised to achieve our destiny of liberation from the problems and attachments of the world. Amida assures that we will all become ripe, ready-to-harvest green rice some day, no matter how poorly planted we may feel ourselves to be.

Issa has a second haiku on green rice that I think completes this thought. Gazing out over the mature rice, he comes to a further realization:

Your rice field,
my rice field—
the same green

The rice doesn't take heed of who planted it—it just grows and becomes green naturally. Someone else's rice may seem better than one's own, or vice versa, but really they're all the same green and all good together. Other Power embraces the worst and the best, and brings all to become the same green. In the Pure Land there are no differences between people, but only mutual support and equal buddhahood. Poorly planted or not, it makes no difference in the end, for we all blossom under the influence of Other Power and become free.

Green rice is a good symbol for the awakened heart. Like green plants, the trusting heart of shinjin is full of life, always fresh, flexible, and rooted in the Vow power that gives us the stability to be

able to bend naturally in the winds of life and right ourselves effortlessly when the wind passes. I know that whenever I pass green rice
while walking in Japan, I think of all the causes and conditions that
contribute to it fulfilling its purpose, and am thankful for those that
support me.

Always Present,
Always Hidden

I N THE WORSHIP HALL at West Los Angeles Buddhist temple (and indeed in many Shin temples) two tassels hang down from the altar in front of the statue, partially obscuring Amida's face.

Though it's rarely mentioned, this is a very important teaching, pointing to one of the deepest mysteries in Shin Buddhism. Amida Buddha embodies true reality in a form accommodated for the understanding of foolish beings such as us. But by partly hiding the buddha's face, the two tassels show us that no matter how much we study, no matter how good we are, no matter how deep our spiritual practice is, the entirety of ultimate reality remains fundamentally beyond all of our capacity for understanding.

Buddhist Dancing

E VERY SUMMER something remarkable happens in American Jodo Shinshu temples. As the days get longer and the heat grows stronger, all the temple activity begins to focus on the upcoming Obon festival. Obon is the primary religious event in Japanese Buddhism. Traditionally it represents the period when the souls of the dead are believed to come back to earth to visit with their loved ones. People clean and beautify the family graves, gossip with their relatives (living and deceased), perform folk dances, and it all culminates with candlelit festivities that send the dead back to their own land for another year.

For Jodo Shinshu, the holiday's significance is that it is a period of remembrance of those who have gone before us, and gratitude toward them and all that have supported us. In America, the focus is especially on the dancing. Obon dancing is a group activity, with everyone gathered in a big circle dancing the same steps in time to the music. Many of the dances actually depict little stories about the lives of common people. Each temple holds

Obon on a different weekend, with practice sessions a couple times a week so that everyone knows the steps. In places with a lot of Shin folks, like southern California, there is an Obon dance going on somewhere nearby every weekend, and people travel from Obon dance to Obon dance week after week, visiting with the other temples and celebrating together. And thus Obon has gone from being a few days in mid-August to being an entire season of fun and togetherness.

I remember one Obon that stands out particularly in my mind. It took place in downtown Los Angeles, at the main temple. Hundreds of people had gathered to eat, chat, play games, and most of all, to dance. As the sun began to go down, the music started and we lined up in the circle. A whole sea of people came together, many wearing colorful Japanese costumes. As we danced, I looked around and saw people from many different Jodo Shinshu temples. And I saw people from the nearby Zen and Vajrayana temples. From previous encounters I knew that there were Christians and Jews there too, as well as people with no particular religion, all dancing.

Around and around we went, laughing and smiling as we went through the different dances. We were white and black, Latino and all sorts of Asian-American, especially Japanese. We were men and women, and great hordes of enthusiastic children. We were priests and laypeople, good and bad, rich and very poor. We were old and we were young, like my son, just five months old, whom I held happily as we danced and danced.

There in the red light of the sun setting out over the Pacific, with the music filling the air and the big *taiko* drums beating, we were a vision of the Pure Land. All people gathered together, all welcome, all unique and all bound as a single group moving as one. No one excluded for color, religion, appearance, class, or any other possible reason. And all dancing the nembutsu in joy, with gratitude and happiness spilling over the crowd like the smell of the traditional foods cooking nearby.

Buddhism can be found in temples, and in books. It can be found in hard meditation and in easy chanting. But for me, there is nothing more wonderful than Buddhist dancing. When you are there in that great gathering of all people, you understand what the stories have been pointing at. And you don't need to meditate, or study the scriptures, or even chant to experience that deepest truth. All you have to do is let faith and thanksgiving well up all by themselves, pick up your feet, and *move*.

Acknowledgments

I WOULD LIKE to thank the staff at Wisdom Publications, especially my editor Josh Bartok, for their hard work on this book. I am also grateful to the people who allowed me to use the various haiku found in the book, especially David Lanoue for his wonderful translations of Issa. I owe many thanks to Rev. Taitetsu Unno for writing the foreword and for his mentorship over the course of many years. I am also thankful to Mark Unno for his work on the foreword. And I am grateful to my wife and son, who always remind me of what is truly important in life.

It would be impossible to count all the people in the Jodo Shinshu community to whom I am indebted for opening the Dharma to me—the best I can do is bow my head and say "Namu Amida Butsu."

Glossary of Terms

Amida: the Japanese name of the Buddha of Boundless Light and Life. In some versions of the story Amida was once a king who, taking bodhisattva vows, practiced until he became a buddha who could free all beings. In other interpretations, Amida represents true reality manifesting itself in a human-like form in order to help those who suffer to achieve liberation.

Ananda: a cousin of the historical Buddha and his attendant monk during the Buddha's later years.

Avalokiteshvara: Indian name of the bodhisattva of great compassion, known in China as Kuan-Yin. Avalokiteshvara is Amida Buddha's helper in saving suffering beings.

Bodhisattva: a being on the way to buddhahood. Some bodhisattvas, such as Avalokiteshvara, are seen as virtually identical to buddhas in wisdom, compassion, and skill at teaching.

Buddha: a person who has fully awoken to the truth of reality and teaches it to others so that they can be freed from their sufferings. In some cases the term buddha is used more abstractly to refer not to a person but to reality itself.

Daiseishi: Japanese name of the wisdom bodhisattva who assists Amida Buddha in liberating deluded beings. Called Mahastamaprapta in Sanskrit.

Dharma: the principles of reality; also, the teachings that conform to that reality or lead to awareness of that reality.

Dharma Storehouse: translated name of the bodhisattva who became Amida Buddha. According to the founding myth of Pure Land Budddhism, Dharma Storehouse made forty-eight vows to create the Pure Land of Bliss and save all beings, then worked for eons until he fulfilled those vows.

Dharmakaya: the universe in its ultimate, liberated state, sometimes personified as an aspect of a buddha.

Honganji: the "Temple of the Primal Vow," founded by Shinran's daughter Kakushinni. Honganji is also the name of the primary lineage (currently with two main branches) that upholds Shinran's teachings.

Jodo Shinshu: "True School of Pure Land," the Buddhist tradition that evolved from Shinran's teachings. Jodo Shinshu is the largest form of Buddhism in Japan.

Jodo Shu: "Pure Land School," the Buddhist tradition that evolved from the teachings of Honen, Shinran's mentor. Jodo Shu is the second largest form of Buddhism in Japan.

Kuan-Yin: Chinese name of Avalokiteshvara, often depicted as a woman.

Kyosei: co-living/symbiosis/shared life. The Pure Land concept of life's interconnectedness, especially in how we recognize our shared living with others and seek to develop harmonious relationships, social justice, and ecological awareness.

Land of Bliss: the name of Amida's Pure Land, mythically represented as existing far to the West. As bliss, it is the opposite of the suffering that we experience when deluded. It is identical with nirvana.

Mahastamaprapta: Indian name of Daiseishi bodhisattva, Amida's helper who personifies wisdom.

Mahayana: "Great Vehicle," a diverse form of Buddhism that focuses on emptiness and the stories of various buddhas and bodhisattvas. Ideas about Amida and the Land of Bliss were part of the earliest developments in Mahayana and helped drive its ascension.

Mara: the personification of evil in Buddhism. Mara is portrayed as a god who rules over those trapped in delusion and thus tries to foil attempts to become liberated.

Myokonin: simple Shin believers whose humility and spontaneity have served as inspiration to other Pure Land practitioners.

Namu Amida Butsu: an expression of devotion and thanksgiving to Amida Buddha, known as the nembutsu. Depending on the context it can be translated as "I take refuge in Amida," "Thank you, Amida," "Praise Amida," or "Help me Amida."

Nembutsu: saying or chanting the name of Amida ("Namu Amida Butsu" is the most common form in Japanese). In different contexts it is a shout of joy, an expression of gratitude, a prayer of deep faith, a cry for help, or a form of remembrance.

Other Power: power-beyond-self, in opposition to ego-bound self-power, which embraces us in our foolishness and frees us. Can be used as a synonym for Amida.

Primal Vow: the eighteenth of Amida's foundational vows, which proclaims that the Pure Land of Bliss was created for all beings.

Pure Land: a basic idea in Mahayana Buddhism, pure lands are realms of liberation that come into being when someone achieves buddhahood. All buddhas have pure lands; the most popular one, often simply called the Pure Land, is Amida's Land of Bliss. Pure Land is also the name of the stream of Buddhism that concerns itself with bringing beings to freedom through the Pure Land.

Sangha: the community of Buddhists, in some interpretations restricted to the monks.

Shakyamuni: title for the historical Buddha, meaning "sage of the Shakya clan." His birth name was Siddhartha Gautama.

Shin: nickname for the Jodo Shinshu tradition of Buddhism.

Shinjin: the trusting heart/mind; also the experience of entrusting in Other Power. For Shin Buddhists, shinjin is the awakening to one's limits and the compassionate embrace of Amida that allows one to live in the Pure Land during this life and receive complete liberation after death.

Shinran: medieval Japanese monk (1173–1262) who created the Jodo Shinshu tradition. He became a monk as a child and practiced for many years before finding true freedom through the Pure Land path. Persecuted by the government for his religious views, he was stripped of his monkhood and sent into exile to die, where he married and managed to attract a large body of followers.

Shunyata: emptiness; the Buddhist acknowledgment of how all things in the universe arise in dependence on each other and thus lack any essential self-nature.

Sutra: Indian name for scriptures considered canonical in the Buddhist tradition.

For Further Reading

Collected Works of Shinran, Volumes I and II, translated by Hongwanji International Center (Jodo Shinshu Hongwanji-ha 1997).

The Essential Shinran, by Alfred Bloom (World Wisdom 2007).

The Great Natural Way, by Hozen Seki (American Buddhist Academy 1976).

Letters of Rennyo, edited by Nagao Gadjin (Hongwanji International Center, 2000).

Letters of the Nun Eshinni, by James Dobbins (University of Hawaii Press 2004).

A Life of Awakening, by Takamaro Shigaraki (Hozokan Publishing 2005).

Living in Amida's Universal Vow, edited by Alfred Bloom (World Wisdom 2004).

The Monk Who Dared, by Ruth Tabrah (Press Pacifica 1995)

The Monk's Wife, by Ruth Tabrah (Buddhist Study Center Press 2001).

Naturalness, by Kenryo Kanamatsu (World Wisdom 2002).

Ocean, by Kenneth Tanaka (Wisdom Ocean Publications 1997).

Pure Land Haiku, by David Lanoue (Buddhist Books International 2004).

River of Fire, River of Water, by Taitetsu Unno (Image 1998).

Shin Buddhism, by Taitetsu Unno (Image 2002).

Shin Sutras to Live By, by Ruth Tabrah and Shoji Matsumoto (Buddhist Study Center Press 1990).

Strategies for Modern Living, by Alfred Bloom (Heian International 1993).

Three Pure Land Sutras, translated by Hisao Inagaki (Numata Center for Buddhist Translation and Research 2003).

Index

About the Authors

Jeff Wilson is an assistant professor of religious studies and East Asian studies, specializing in Buddhist traditions, both Asian and North American. He has previously published *The Buddhist Guide to New York* and *Mourning the Unborn Dead: A Buddhist Ritual Comes to America* and is a contributing editor for the Buddhist magazine *Tricycle*. He lives with his family in Canada.

Mark Unno is Associate Professor of Japanese Buddhism at the University of Oregon. He is also an ordained minister in the Shin Buddhist tradition, and the author of numerous articles and several books. Mark and his father Taitetsu Unno have led a course on Shin Buddhism at the Barre Center for Buddhist Studies, and they were also keynote speakers for the Centennial Celebration of the Buddhist Churches of America, the main organization for Shin Buddhism in the United States.

Taitetsu Unno is the Jill Ker Conway Professor Emeritus of Religion at Smith College. Recognized as one of the foremost teachers of Shin Buddhism in the United States, he is a Shin priest and author of *River of Fire, River of Water: An Introduction to the Pure Land Tradition of Shin Buddhism* and *Shin Buddhism: Bits of Rubble Turn into Gold*. He lives in Eugene, Oregon.

About Wisdom Publications

Wisdom Publications, a nonprofit publisher, is dedicated to making available authentic works relating to Buddhism for the benefit of all. We publish books by ancient and modern masters in all traditions of Buddhism, translations of important texts, and original scholarship. Additionally, we offer books that explore East-West themes unfolding as traditional Buddhism encounters our modern culture in all its aspects. Our titles are published with the appreciation of Buddhism as a living philosophy, and with the special commitment to preserve and transmit important works from Buddhism's many traditions.

To learn more about Wisdom, or to browse books online, visit our website at www.wisdompubs.org.

You may request a copy of our catalog online or by writing to this address:

Wisdom Publications
199 Elm Street
Somerville, Massachusetts 02144 USA
Telephone: 617-776-7416
Fax: 617-776-7841
Email: info@wisdompubs.org
www.wisdompubs.org

The Wisdom Trust

As a nonprofit publisher, Wisdom is dedicated to the publication of Dharma books for the benefit of all sentient beings and dependent upon the kindness and generosity of sponsors in order to do so. If you would like to make a donation to Wisdom, you may do so through our website or our Somerville office. If you would like to help sponsor the publication of a book, please write or email us at the address above.

Thank you.

Wisdom is a nonprofit, charitable 501(c)(3) organization affiliated with the Foundation for the Preservation of the Mahayana Tradition (FPMT).